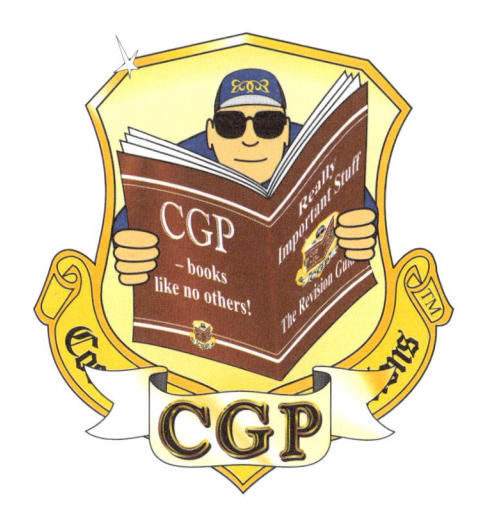

It's another Quality Book from CGP

This book is for anyone doing AQA Coordinated Science at GCSE.

Whatever subject you're doing it's the same old story — there are lots of facts and you've just got to learn them. AQA Coordinated Science is no different.

Happily this CGP book gives you all that important information as clearly and concisely as possible.

It's also got some daft bits in to try and make the whole experience at least vaguely entertaining for you.

Higher — This book is suitable for both Higher and Foundation Tier candidates. The material which is required only for higher tier is clearly indicated in blue boxes like this. In addition, the Higher Tier questions in the Revision Summaries are printed in blue. — *Higher*

What CGP is all about

Our sole aim here at CGP is to produce the highest quality books — carefully written, immaculately presented and dangerously close to being funny.

Then we work our socks off to get them out to you — at the cheapest possible prices.

Contents

Section One — Electricity

(AQA Syllabus Reference)

- *(12.1) Potential Difference in Circuits*
  - Circuits — The Basics 1
  - Resistance and V = I×R 2
  - Circuit Symbols and Devices 3
  - Series Circuits 4
  - Parallel Circuits 6
- *(12.2) Energy in Circuits*
  - Energy in Circuits 8
- *(12.3) Mains Electricity*
  - Mains Electricity 9
  - Fuses and Earthing 10
- *(12.4) The Cost of Using Electrical Appliances*
  - Domestic Electricity 11
- *(12.5) Electric Charge*
  - Static Electricity 12
  - Static Electricity — Examples 13
  - Electrolysis 14
  - Revision Summary For Section One 15

Section Two — Forces and Motion

(AQA Syllabus Reference)

- *(12.6) Representing & Measuring Motion*
  - Mass, Weight and Gravity 16
- *(12.7) Forces and Acceleration*
  - Velocity and Acceleration 17
  - D-T and V-T Graphs 18
  - The Three Laws of Motion 19
  - Force Diagrams 21
  - Terminal Velocity 22
- *(12.8) Frictional Forces & Non-Uniform Motion*
  - Friction 23
  - Stopping Distances for Cars 24
  - Revision Summary for Section Two 25

Section Three — Waves

(AQA Syllabus Reference)

- *(12.9) Characteristics of Waves*
  - Waves — Basic Principles 26
  - Reflection 27
  - Refraction 28
  - Refraction: Two Special Cases 29
  - Total Internal Reflection 30
  - Diffraction 31
  - Using s = d/t and v = fλ 32
- *(12.10) The Electromagnetic Spectrum*
  - The E.M. Spectrum 33
  - Microwaves and Infrared 34
  - Visible, UV, X-rays, γ-Rays 35
  - Digital and Analogue Signals 36
- *(12.11) Sound and Ultrasound*
  - Sound Waves 37
  - Frequency and Ultrasound 38
  - Ultrasonic Detection 39
  - The Speed of Sound 40
- *(12.12) Seismic Waves*
  - Seismic Waves 41
- *(12.13) Tectonics*
  - Evidence for Plate Tectonics 42
  - Plate Boundaries 43
  - Revision Summary for Section Three 45

Section Four — The Earth and Beyond

(AQA Syllabus Reference)

- *(12.14) The Solar System* .....
  - The Cause of Days and Seasons 46
  - The Solar System 47
  - The Planets 48
  - Satellites 49
  - Satellites and Comets 50
- *(12.15) The Universe* .....
  - The Universe 51
  - The Life Cycle of Stars 52
  - Searching for Life on Other Planets 53
  - The Origin of the Universe 54
  - The Future of the Universe 55
  - Revision Summary for Section Four 56

Section Five — Energy Resources & Energy Transfer

(AQA Syllabus Reference)

- *(12.16) Thermal Energy Transfer* .....
  - Energy Transfer 57
  - Heat Transfer 58
  - Conduction of Heat 59
  - Convection of Heat 60
  - Heat Radiation 61
  - Applications of Heat Transfer 62
  - Keeping Buildings Warm 63
  - Useful Energy Transfers 64
- *(12.17) Efficiency* .....
  - Efficiency of Machines 65
- *(12.18) Energy Resources* .....
  - Sources of Power 66
  - Power from Non-Renewables 67
  - Power from Renewables 68
- *(12.19) Work, Power and Energy* .....
  - Work Done, Energy and Power 70
  - Kinetic and Potential Energy 71
  - K.E. and P.E. — Some Examples 72
- *(12.20) Electromagnetic Forces* .....
  - Magnetic Fields 73
  - Electromagnets 74
  - The Motor Effect 75
  - Electromagnetic Devices 76
- *(12.21) Electromagnetic Induction* .....
  - Electromagnetic Induction 77
  - Transformers 78
  - The National Grid 79
  - Revision Summary for Section Five 80

Section Six — Radioactivity

(AQA Syllabus Reference)

- *(12.22) Types & Properties and uses of Radioactivity.*
  - Types of Radiation 81
  - Background Radiation 82
  - Radiation Hazards and Safety 83
  - Uses of Radioactive Materials 84
- *(12.23) Atomic Structure & Nuclear Fission* .....
  - Atomic Structure 85
  - Nuclear Fission 86
  - Half-life 87
  - Revision Summary for Section Six 88

- Answers 88
- Index 89

Published by Coordination Group Publications Ltd.
Illustrations by :Sandy Gardner, e-mail: illustrations@sandygardner.co.uk
and Bowser, Colorado USA

Updated by:
Chris Dennett
Tim Major
Becky May
Katherine Reed

ISBN 1-84146-960-2

Groovy website: www.cgpbooks.co.uk

Printed by Elanders Hindson, Newcastle upon Tyne.
Clipart sources: CorelDRAW and VECTOR.

Text, design, layout and original illustrations © Richard Parsons 2002
All rights reserved.

Section One — Electricity

Circuits — The Basics

Potential Difference in Circuits

Isn't electricity great. Mind you it's pretty bad news if the words don't mean anything to you... Hey, I know — learn them now!

1) **CURRENT** is the *flow* of electrons round the circuit. Current will *only flow* through a component if there is a *voltage* across that component.

2) **VOLTAGE** is the *driving force* that pushes the current round. Kind of like *"electrical pressure"*.

3) **RESISTANCE** is anything in the circuit which *slows the flow down*.

4) **THERE'S A BALANCE**: the *voltage* is trying to *push* the current round the circuit, and the *resistance* is *opposing* it — the *relative sizes* of the voltage and resistance decide *how big* the current will be:

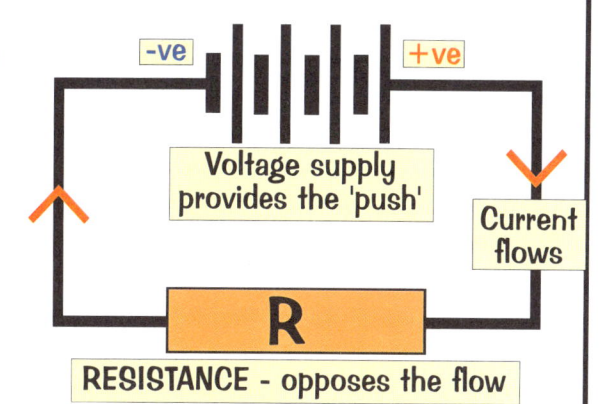

> If you *increase the VOLTAGE* — then **MORE CURRENT** will flow.
> If you *increase the RESISTANCE* — then **LESS CURRENT** will flow
> (or **MORE VOLTAGE** will be needed to keep the **SAME CURRENT** flowing).

Voltage supply provides the 'push'
Current flows
RESISTANCE - opposes the flow

The Standard Test Circuit

This is without doubt the most totally dog-standard circuit the world has ever known. So know it.

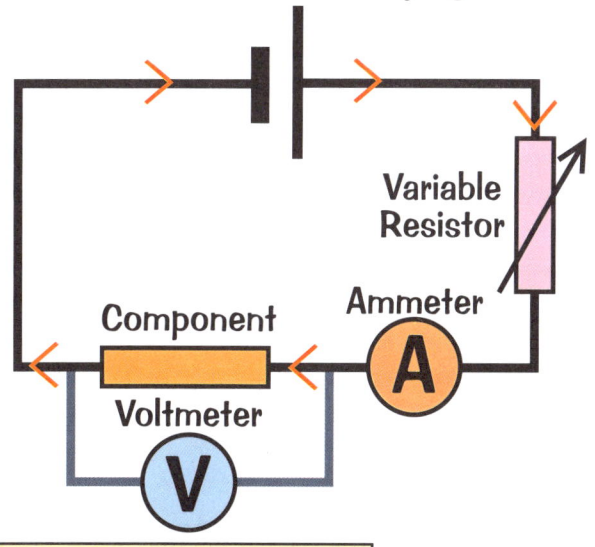

The Ammeter
1) Measures the *current* (in *amps*) flowing through the component.
2) Must be placed *in series*.
3) Can be put *anywhere* in series in the *main circuit*, but *never* in parallel like the voltmeter.

The Voltmeter
1) Measures the *voltage* (in *volts*) across the component.
2) Must be placed *in parallel* around the *component* under test — *NOT* around the variable resistor or the battery!
3) The *proper* name for *"voltage"* is *"potential difference"* or *"Pd"*.

Five Important Points

1) This *very basic* circuit is used for testing *components*, and for getting *V-I graphs* for them.
2) The *component*, the *ammeter* and the *variable resistor* are all in *series*, which means they can be put in *any order* in the main circuit. The *voltmeter*, on the other hand, can only be placed *in parallel* around the *component under test*, as shown. Anywhere else is a definite *no-no*.
3) As you *vary* the *variable resistor* it alters the *current* flowing through the circuit.
4) This allows you to take several **PAIRS OF READINGS** from the *ammeter* and *voltmeter*.
5) You can then *plot* these values for *current* and *voltage* on a *V-I graph* (See next page).

Understanding circuits — easy as pie...

This page is all about electric circuits — what they are, how to use them, and how they work. This is the most basic stuff on electricity there is. I assume you realise that you'll never be able to learn anything else about electricity until you know this stuff — don't you? Good-oh.

Resistance and V=I×R

Potential Difference in Circuits

Four Hideously Important Voltage-Current Graphs

V-I graphs show how the current varies as you change the voltage. Learn these four real well:

Resistor — straight line through origin (I vs V)

Different Wires — multiple straight lines through origin with different slopes

Filament Lamp — S-shaped curve through origin

Diode — current flows only in one direction (curve in positive V region)

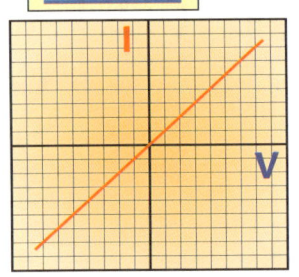

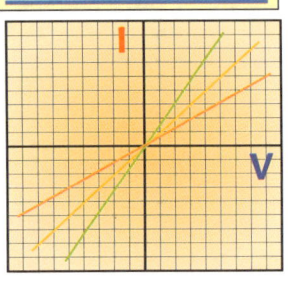

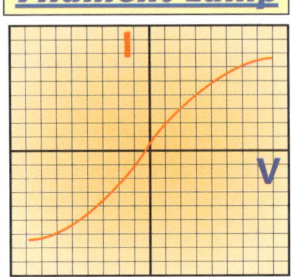

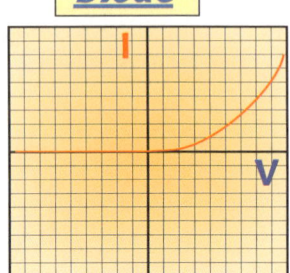

Explaining the graphs above:

Resistor
The current through a RESISTOR (at constant temperature) is *proportional to voltage*.

Different Wires
Different wires have different *resistances*, hence the different *slopes*.

Filament Lamp
As the *temperature* of the filament *increases*, the *resistance increases*, hence the *curve*.

Diode
Current will only flow through a diode *in one direction*, as shown.

Calculating Resistance: R = V/I, (or R = "1/gradient")

For the *straight-line graphs* the resistance of the component is *steady* and is equal to the *inverse* of the *gradient* of the line, or *"1/gradient"*. In other words, the *STEEPER* the graph the *LOWER* the resistance.

If the graph *curves*, it means the resistance is *changing*. In that case R can be found for any point by taking the *pair of values* (V,I) from the graph and sticking them in the formula R = V/I. Easy.

$$\text{Resistance} = \frac{\text{Potential Difference}}{\text{Current}}$$

$$\frac{V}{I \times R}$$

Calculating Resistance — An Example

EXAMPLE. Voltmeter V reads 6V and resistor R is 4Ω, what is the current through Ammeter A?

ANSWER. Taking the formula V = I×R, we need to find I so the version we need is I = V/R. The answer is then: 6/4 which is 1½ A.

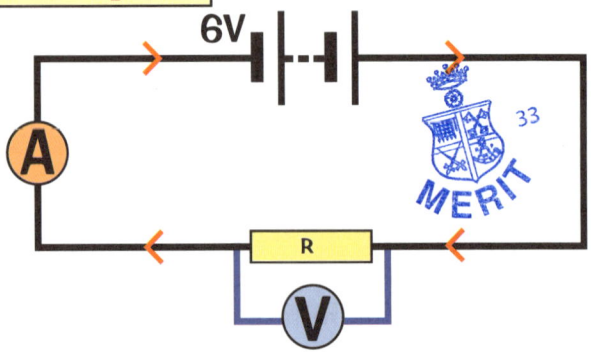

In the end, you'll have to learn this — resistance is futile...

There are quite a lot of important details on this page and you need to *learn all of them*. The only way to make sure you really know it is to *cover up the page* and see how much of it you can *scribble down* from *memory*. Sure, it's not that easy — but it's the only way. Enjoy.

AQA Syllabus Section One — Electricity

Circuit Symbols and Devices

Potential Difference in Circuits

Circuit Symbols You Should Know:

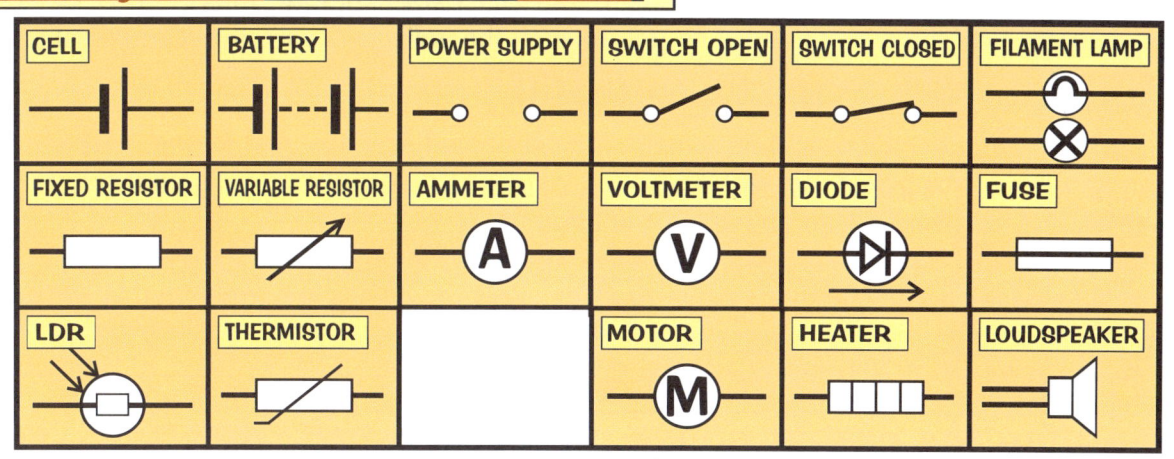

CELL	BATTERY	POWER SUPPLY	SWITCH OPEN	SWITCH CLOSED	FILAMENT LAMP
FIXED RESISTOR	VARIABLE RESISTOR	AMMETER	VOLTMETER	DIODE	FUSE
LDR	THERMISTOR		MOTOR	HEATER	LOUDSPEAKER

1) Variable Resistor

1) A *resistor* whose resistance can be *changed* by twiddling a knob or something.
2) The old-fashioned ones are huge coils of *wire* with a *slider* on them.
3) They're great for *altering* the current flowing through a circuit.
   Turn the resistance *up*, the current *drops*. Turn the resistance *down*, the current goes *up*.

2) "Semiconductor Diode" or just "Diode"

A special device made from *semiconductor* material such as *silicon*.
It lets current flow freely through it in *one direction*, but *not* in the other
(i.e. there's a very high resistance in the *reverse* direction).
This turns out to be real useful in various *electronic circuits*.

3) Light Dependent Resistor or "LDR" to you

1) In *bright light*, the resistance *falls*.
2) In *darkness*, the resistance is *highest*.
3) This makes it a useful device for various
   electronic circuits e.g. *automatic night lights*;
   burglar detectors.

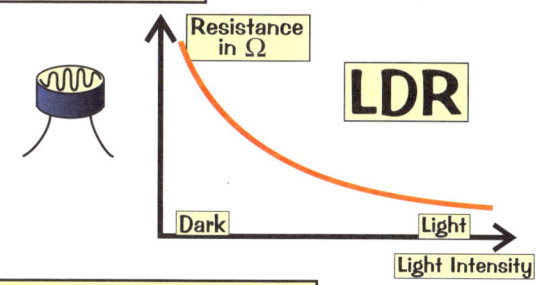

4) Thermistor (Temperature-dependent Resistor)

1) In *hot* conditions, the resistance *drops*.
2) In *cool* conditions, the resistance goes *up*.
3) Thermistors make useful *temperature detectors*, e.g. *car engine* temperature sensors and electronic *thermostats*.

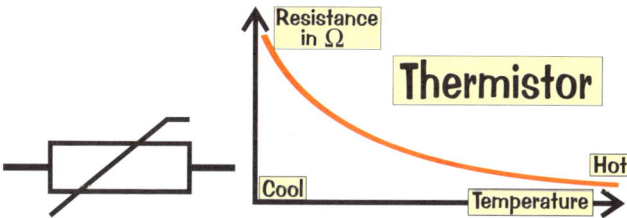

"Diode" — wasn't that a film starring Bruce Willis...

Another page of basic but important details about electrical circuits. You need to know all those circuit symbols as well as the extra details for the four special devices. When you think you know it all try *covering the page* and *scribbling it all down*. See how you did, and *then try again*.

Section One — Electricity · AQA Syllabus

Series Circuits

Potential Difference in Circuits

You need to be able to tell the difference between series and parallel circuits *just by looking at them*. You also need to know the *rules* about what happens with both types. Read on.

Series Circuits — all or nothing

1) In *series circuits*, the different components are connected *in a line*, *end to end*, between the +ve and −ve of the power supply (except for *voltmeters*, which are always connected *in parallel*, but they don't count as part of the circuit).
2) If you remove or disconnect *one* component, the circuit is *broken* and they all *stop*.
3) This is generally *not very handy*, and in practice, *very few things* are connected in series.

1) Potential Difference is Shared:

1) In series circuits the *total Pd* of the *supply* is *shared* between the various *components*
2) The *voltages* round a series circuit *always add up* to equal the *source voltage*:

$$V = V_1 + V_2 + V_3$$

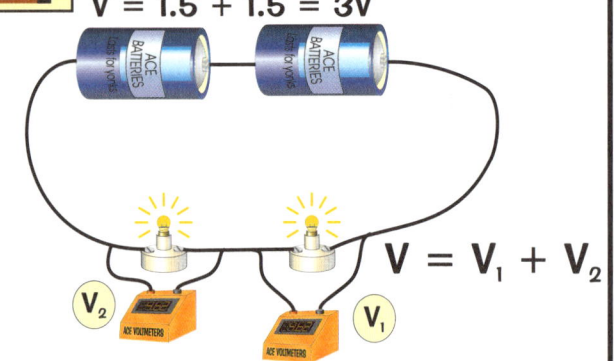

$V = 1.5 + 1.5 = 3V$

$V = V_1 + V_2$

2) Current is the Same everywhere:

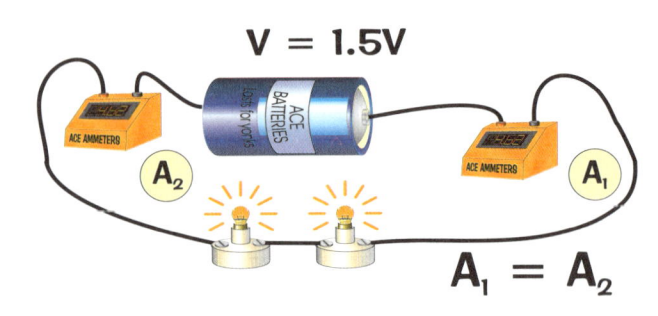

$V = 1.5V$

1) In series circuits the *same current* flows through *all parts* of the circuit. i.e. The reading on ammeter A_1 is the same as the reading on ammeter A_2:

$$A_1 = A_2$$

$A_1 = A_2$

2) The *size* of the current is determined by the *total Pd* of the cells and the *total resistance* of the circuit: i.e. $I = V/R$

3) Resistance Adds Up:

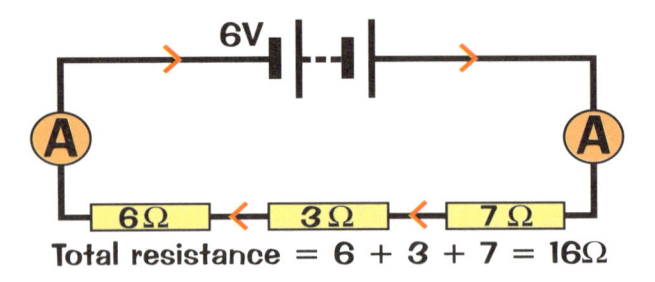

1) In series circuits the *total resistance* is just the *sum* of all the resistances:

$$R = R_1 + R_2 + R_3$$

6V

6Ω   3Ω   7Ω
Total resistance = 6 + 3 + 7 = 16Ω

2) The *bigger* the *resistance* of a component, the bigger its *share* of the *total Pd*.

AQA Syllabus

Section One — Electricity

Series Circuits — Potential Difference in Circuits

Cell voltages add up:

1) There is a bigger potential difference with more cells in series, provided the cells are all *connected* the *same way*.
2) For example when two batteries of voltage 1.5V are *connected in series* they supply 3V *between them*.

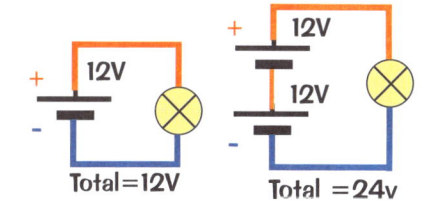

Total = 12V   Total = 24v

More Lamps in series means Dimmer Lamps:

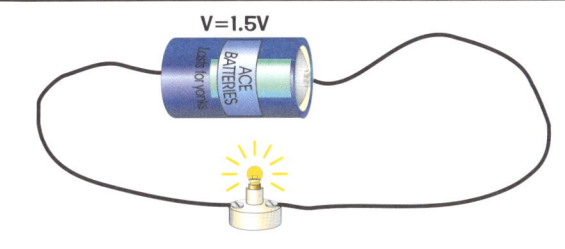

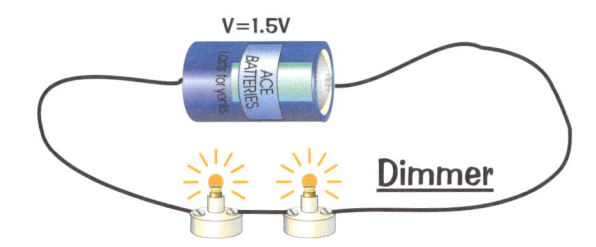

V = 1.5V

V = 1.5V   Dimmer

1) If a *lamp* is connected in series with a battery then it lights up with a certain brightness.
2) However with *more lamps* (of the same resistance) connected in series then all the lamps will light up at a *reduced brightness*.
3) This is because in a *series circuit* the voltage is *shared out* between the components in the circuit.
4) When a *second cell* is connected in series with the first then the brightness of the lamps will *increase* because there is a bigger source P.d.

Example on series circuits

With the circuit opposite the rules on these two pages apply:

Voltages add to equal the *source voltage*:
1.5 + 2 + 2.5 = 6V

Total resistance is the sum of the resistances in the circuit: 3 + 4 + 5 = 12 ohms

Current flowing through all parts of the circuit = V/R = 6/12 = 0.5A

(If an extra cell was added of voltage 3V then the voltage across each resistor would increase.)

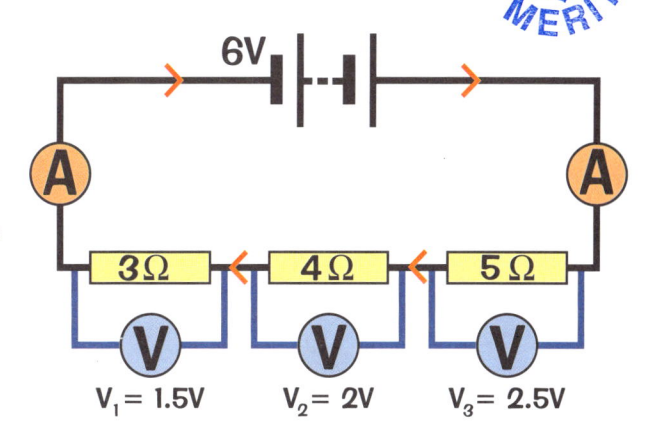

V_1 = 1.5V V_2 = 2V V_3 = 2.5V

Christmas Fairy Lights are Wired in Series

Christmas fairy lights are about the *only* real-life example of things connected in *series*, and we all know what a *pain* they are when the *whole lot go out* just because *one* of the bulbs is slightly dicky. The only *advantage* is that the bulbs can be *very small* because the total 230V is *shared out* between them, so each bulb only has a *small* voltage across it.

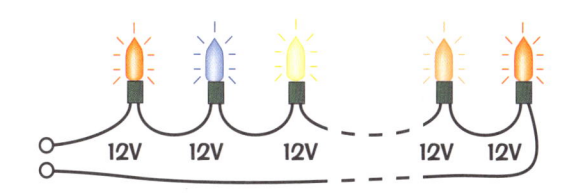

Series Circuits — phew, it's just one thing after another...

They really do want you to know the difference between series and parallel circuits. It's not that tricky but you do have to make a real effort to *learn all the details*. That's what these pages are for. Learn all those details, then *cover the pages* and *scribble them all down*. Then try again...

Section One — Electricity   AQA Syllabus

Parallel Circuits

Potential Difference in Circuits

Parallel circuits are much more *sensible* than series circuits and so they're much more *common* in *real life*.

Parallel Circuits — Independence and Isolation

1) In *parallel circuits*, each component is *separately* connected to the +ve and –ve of the *supply*.
2) If you remove or disconnect *one* of them, it will *hardly affect* the others at all.
3) This is *obviously* how *most* things must be connected, for example in *cars* and in *household electrics*. You have to be able to switch everything on and off *separately*.

P.D. is the Same across all components:

1) In parallel circuits *all* components get the *full source Pd*, so the voltage is the *same* across all components:

$$V_1 = V_2 = V_3$$

2) This means that *identical bulbs* connected in parallel will all be at the *same brightness*. This is totally different from bulbs connected in series.

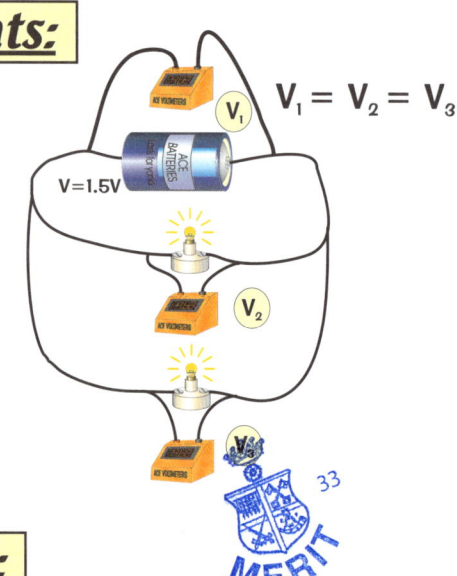

Current is Shared between branches:

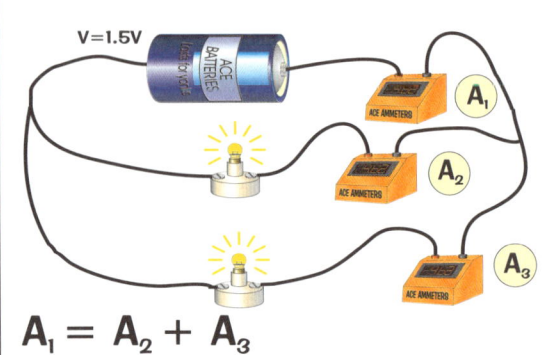

1) In parallel circuits the *total current* flowing around the circuit is equal to the *total* of all the currents in the *separate branches*.

$$A = A_1 + A_2 + A_3$$

$A_1 = A_2 + A_3$

2) In a parallel circuit, there are *junctions* where the current either *splits* or *rejoins*. The total current going *into* a junction *always* equals the total currents *leaving* — fairly obviously.

3) If two *identical components* are connected in parallel then the *same current* will flow through each component.

Resistance Is Tricky:

1) The *current* through each component depends on its *resistance*. The *lower* the resistance, the *bigger* the current that'll flow through it.
2) The *total resistance* of the circuit is *tricky to work out*, but it's always *LESS* than the branch with the *smallest* resistance.

Parallel Circuits

Potential Difference in Circuits

Parallel Circuits Example

1) The *voltage* across each resistor in the circuit is the same as the *supply voltage*. Each voltmeter will read 6V.

2) The current through each resistor will be *different* because they have different values of *resistance*.

3) The current through the battery is the same as the *sum* of the other currents in the branches.
 i.e. $A_1 = A_2 + A_3 + A_4$
 $A_1 = 1.5 + 3 + 1 = 5.5A$

4) The *total resistance* in the whole circuit is *less* than the *lowest branch*, i.e. lower than 2Ω.

5) The *biggest current* flows through the *middle branch* because that branch has the *lowest resistance*.

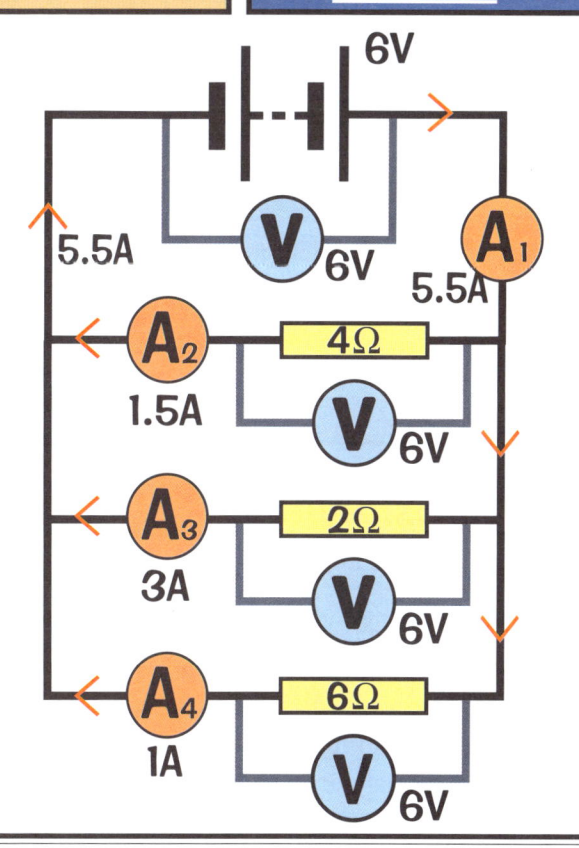

Everything Electrical in a Car is Connected in Parallel

Parallel connection is *essential* in a car to give these *two features*:

1) Everything can be *turned on and off separately*.
2) Everything always gets the *full voltage* from the battery.

The only *slight effect* is that when you turn *lots of things on* the lights may go *dim* because the battery can't provide *full voltage* under *heavy load*. This is normally a *very slight* effect. You can spot the same thing at home when you turn a kettle on, if you watch very carefully.

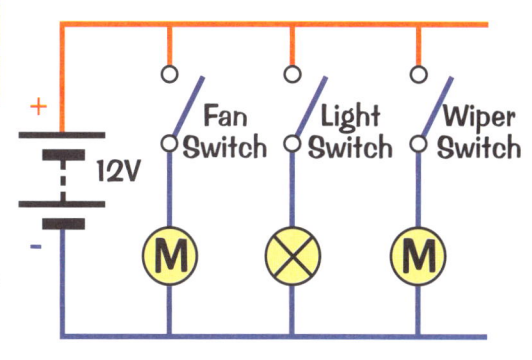

Voltmeters and Ammeters are Exceptions to the rule:

1) Ammeters and Voltmeters are *exceptions* to the series and parallel rules.
2) Ammeters are *always* connected in *series* even in a parallel circuit.
3) Voltmeters are *always* connected in *parallel with a component* even in a series circuit.

Electric Circuits — unparalleled dreariness...

Make sure you can scribble down a parallel circuit and know what the advantages are. Learn the five numbered points and the details for connecting ammeters and voltmeters, and also what two features make parallel connection essential in a car. Then *cover the page* and *scribble it*...

Section One — Electricity
AQA Syllabus

Energy in Circuits

You can look at _electrical circuits_ in _two ways_. The first is in terms of a voltage _pushing the current_ round and the resistances opposing the flow, as on P. 1. The _other way_ of looking at circuits is in terms of _energy transfer_. Learn them _both_ and be ready to tackle questions about _either_.

Energy _is_ Transferred from Cells and Other Sources

Anything which _supplies electricity_ is also supplying _energy_. So cells, batteries, generators etc. all _transfer energy_ to components in the circuit. _Learn these as examples_:

MOTION: motors   **LIGHT:** light bulbs   **HEAT:** Hairdriers/kettles   **SOUND:** speakers

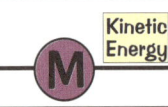

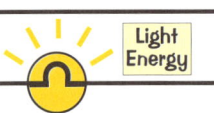

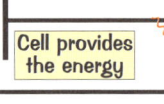

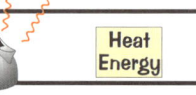

All Resistors produce Heat when a Current flows through them

1) This is important. Whenever a _current_ flows through anything with _electrical resistance_ (which is pretty well _everything_) then _electrical energy_ is converted into _heat energy_.
2) The _more current_ that flows, the _more heat_ is produced.

Calculating Electrical Power and Fuse ratings

1) The standard formula for electrical power is: P = V × I
2) Most electrical goods indicate their _power rating_ and _voltage rating_. To work out the **FUSE** needed, you need to work out the _current_ that the item will normally use. That means using "P=VI", or rather, "I=P/V".

   EXAMPLE: A hairdrier is rated at 240V, 1.1kW. Find the fuse needed.
   ANSWER: I = P/V = 1100/240 = 4.6A. Normally, the fuse should be rated just a little higher than the normal current, so a 5 amp fuse is ideal for this one.

Charge, Voltage and Energy Change

1) Current is the _flow of electrical charge_ around a circuit. When _current_ (I) flows past a point in a circuit for a length of _time_ (t) then _charge_ (Q) has passed. This is given by the formula: **Q = It**
   More charge passes around the circuit when a _bigger current_ flows.

2) When electrical _charge_ (Q) goes through a _change_ in voltage (V), then _energy_ (E) is _transferred_.
   Energy is _supplied_ to the charge at the _power source_ to raise it through a voltage.
   The charge _gives up_ this energy when it _falls_ through any _voltage drop_ in _components_ elsewhere in the circuit.
   The formula is real simple: **E = QV**

3) The _bigger_ the _change_ in voltage (or PD), the _more energy_ is transferred for a _given amount of charge_ passing through the circuit. That means that a battery with a _bigger voltage_ will supply _more energy_ to the circuit for every _coulomb_ of charge which flows round it, because the charge is raised up "_higher_" at the start (see above diagram) — and as the diagram shows, _more energy_ will be _dissipated_ in the circuit too.

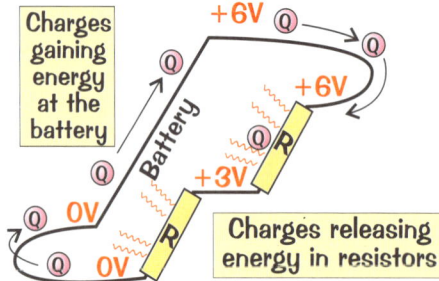

Electricity — why does it all turn out so dreary ...

I try to make it interesting, really I do. I mean, underneath it all, electricity is pretty good stuff, but somehow every page just seems to end up stuffed full of interminably dreary facts. Well look, _I tried_, OK. It may be dreary but you've just gotta _learn it all_, and that's that.

AQA Syllabus   Section One — Electricity

Mains Electricity

Now then, did you know... electricity is dangerous. It can kill you. Well just watch out for it, that's all.

Hazards in The Home — Eliminate Them before They Eliminate You

A likely Exam question will show you a picture of domestic bliss but with various electrical hazards in the picture such as kids shoving their fingers into sockets and stuff like that, and they'll ask you to list all the hazards. This should be mostly common sense, but it won't half help if you already know some of the likely hazards, so learn these 9 examples:

1) Long cables.
2) Frayed cables.
3) Cables in contact with something hot or wet.
4) Water near sockets.
5) Shoving things into sockets.
6) Damaged plugs.
7) Too many plugs into one socket.
8) Lighting sockets without bulbs in.
9) Appliances without their covers on.

Plugs and Cables — Learn the Safety Features

Get the Wiring Right:

1) The right coloured wire to each pin, and firmly screwed in.
2) No bare wires showing inside the plug.
3) Cable grip tightly fastened over the cable outer layer.

Plug Features:

1) The metal parts are made of copper or brass because these are very good conductors.
2) The case, cable grip and cable insulation are all made of plastic because this is a really good insulator and is flexible too.
3) This all keeps the electricity flowing where it should.

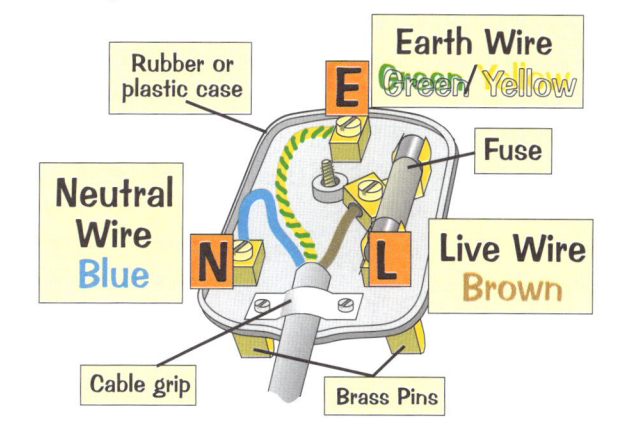

Earth Wire — Green/Yellow
Neutral Wire — Blue
Live Wire — Brown
Rubber or plastic case, Fuse, Cable grip, Brass Pins

Plug Wiring Errors

They're pretty keen on these diagrams in the Exam so make sure you know them. The diagram above shows how to wire a plug properly. Shown below are examples of how not to wire a plug. A badly wired plug is real dangerous so learn these diagrams.

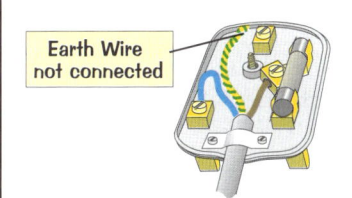

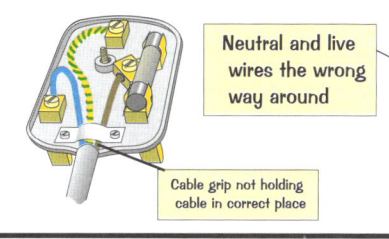

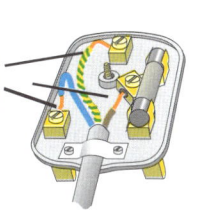

- Earth Wire not connected
- Cable grip not holding cable in correct place
- Neutral and live wires the wrong way around
- Bare wires showing

Some people are so careless with electricity — it's shocking...

Make sure you can list all those hazards in the home. Make sure you know all the details for wiring a plug. Trickiest of all, make sure you can spot when a plug is not wired properly and how to fix it. Learnt it all? Good-O. So cover the page and scribble it all down again.

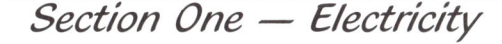

Section One — Electricity   AQA Syllabus

Fuses and Earthing

Mains Electricity

Mains Supply is AC, Battery supply is DC

1) The UK mains supply is approximately 230 volts.
2) It is an AC supply (alternating current), which means the current is constantly changing direction.
3) The frequency of the AC mains supply is 50 cycles per second or 50Hz.
4) By contrast, cells and batteries supply direct current (DC). This just means that the current keeps flowing in the same direction.

Fuses prevent Electric Shocks

1) To prevent surges of current in electrical circuits and danger of electric shocks, a fuse (or circuit breaker see P.77) is normally placed in the circuit.
2) If the current in the circuit gets too big (bigger than the fuse rating), the fuse wire heats up and the fuse blows breaking the circuit thus preventing any electric shocks.
3) Fuses should be rated as near as possible but just higher than the normal operating current.
4) The fuse should always be the same value as the manufacturer recommends.

Earthing prevents Fires and Shocks

The LIVE WIRE in a mains supply alternates between a HIGH +VE AND −VE VOLTAGE. The NEUTRAL WIRE is always at 0V. Electricity normally flows in and out through the live and neutral wires only. The EARTH WIRE and fuse (or circuit breaker See P.77) are just for safety and work together like this:

1) The earth pin is connected to the case via the earth wire (The yellow and green wire).
2) If a fault develops in which the live somehow touches the metal case, then because the case is earthed, a big current flows in through the live, through the case and out down the earth wire.
3) This surge in current blows the fuse (or trips the circuit breaker), which cuts off the live supply. This prevents electric shocks from the case.

All appliances with metal cases must be "earthed" to avoid the danger of electric shock. "Earthing" just means the metal case must be attached to the earth wire in the cable.

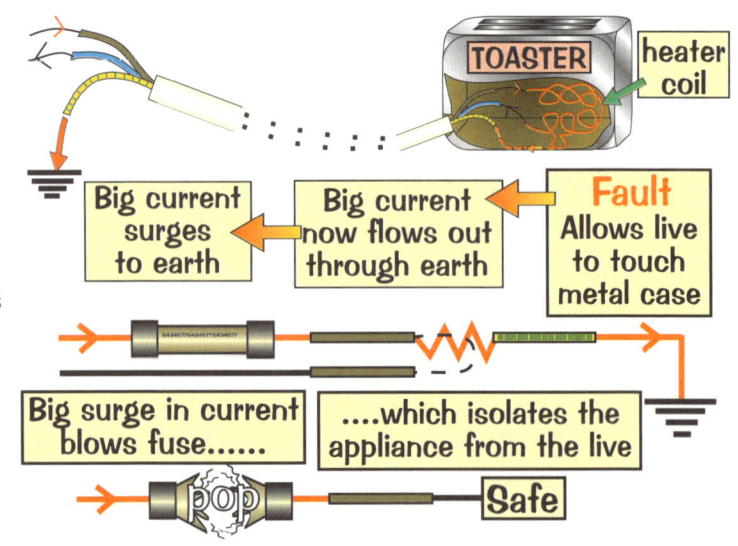

Mains Supply and Fuses — what on Earth is it all about...

Well there you go, three important sections rolled onto one page. Make sure you remember the important formula in the middle there. Learn the details under each heading, cover up the page and scribble it down. If you don't get it the first time check back and try again.

AQA Syllabus

Section One — Electricity

Domestic Electricity

The Cost of Using Electrical Appliances

Electricity is by far the most _useful_ form of energy. Compared to gas or oil or coal etc. it's _much easier_ to turn it into the _four_ main types of useful energy: _Heat_, _light_, _sound_ and _motion_.

Reading Your Electricity Meter and Working out the Bill

Yip, this is in the syllabus. Don't ask me why, because you never actually need to bother in real life!

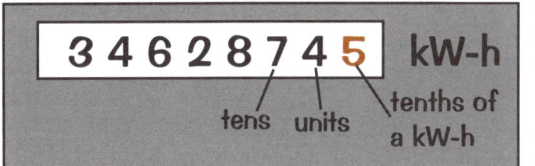

`3 4 6 2 8 7 4 5` kW-h
(tens, units, tenths of a kW-h)

The reading on your meter shows the _total number of units_ (kW-h) used since the meter was fitted. Each bill is worked out from the _INCREASE_ in the meter reading since it was _last read_ for the previous bill.

Kilowatt-hours (kW-h) are "UNITS" of Energy

1) Your electricity meter counts the number of "UNITS" used. A "UNIT" is otherwise known as a _kilowatt-hour_, or _kW-h_. A "kW-h" might sound like a unit of power, but it's not — it's an _amount of energy_.

> A _KILOWATT-HOUR_ is the amount of electrical energy used by a _1 kW APPLIANCE_ left on for _1 HOUR_.

$\frac{E}{P \times t}$

2) Make sure you can turn _1 kW-h_ into _3,600,000 joules_ like this:
"E=P×t" = 1kW × 1 hour = 1000W × 3,600 secs = _3,600,000 J_ (= 3.6 MJ)
(The formula is "Energy = Power×time", and the units must be converted to SI first).

The Two Easy Formulae for Calculating The Cost of Electricity

These must surely be the two most _trivial and obvious_ formulae you'll ever see:

| No. of _UNITS_ (kW-h) used = _POWER_ (in kW) × _TIME_ (in hours) | Units = kW × hours |

| _COST_ = No. of _UNITS_ × _PRICE_ per UNIT | Cost = Units × Price |

N.B. Always turn the _power_ into _kW_ (not watts) and the _time_ into _hours_ (not minutes)

Power Ratings of Appliances

A light bulb converts _electrical energy_ into _light_ and has a power rating of 100W which means it transfers _100 joules/second_.

A kettle converts _electrical energy_ into _heat_ and has a power rating of 3kW, transferring _3000 joules/second_.

The total amount of energy transferred by an appliance therefore depends on _how long_ the appliance is on and its _power rating_ (E=P×t). For example the kettle is on for an hour the energy transferred by the kettle in this time is 3600×3000 = 10800 kJ (3600s = 1 hour).

Kilowa Towers — the Best Lit Hotel in Hawaii...

This page has four sections and you need to learn the stuff in all of them. Start by memorising the headings, then learn the details under each heading. Then _cover the page_ and _scribble down_ what you know. Check back and see what you missed, and then _try again_. And keep trying.

Static Electricity

Electric Charge

Static electricity is all about charges which are _NOT_ free to move. This causes them to build up in one place and it often ends with a _spark_ or a _shock_ when they do finally move.

1) Build up of Static is Caused by Friction

1) When two _insulating_ materials are _rubbed_ together, electrons will be _scraped off one_ and _dumped_ on the other.
2) This'll leave a _positive_ static charge on one and a _negative_ static charge on the other.
3) _Which way_ the electrons are transferred _depends_ on the _two materials_ involved.
4) Electrically charged objects _attract_ small objects placed near them.
   (Try this: rub a balloon on a woolly pully – then put it near tiddly bits of paper and watch them jump.)
5) The classic examples are _polythene_ and _acetate_ rods being rubbed with a _cloth duster_, as shown in the diagrams:

With the _polythene rod_, electrons move _from the duster_ to the rod.

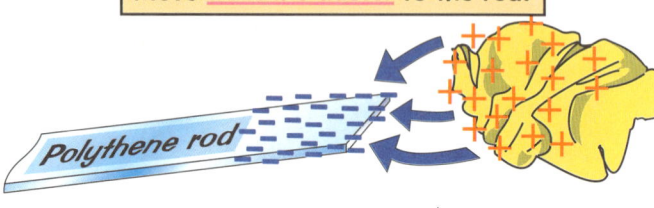

With the _acetate rod_, electrons move _from the rod_ to the duster.

2) Only Electrons Move — Never the Positive Charges

Watch out for this in Exams. Both +ve and –ve electrostatic charges are only ever produced by the movement of _electrons_. The positive charges _definitely do not move_! A positive static charge is always caused by electrons _moving_ away elsewhere, as shown above. Don't forget!

A charged conductor can be _discharged safely_ by connecting it to earth with a _metal strap_. The electrons flow _down_ the strap to the ground if the charge is _negative_ and flow _up_ the strap from the ground if the charge is _positive_.

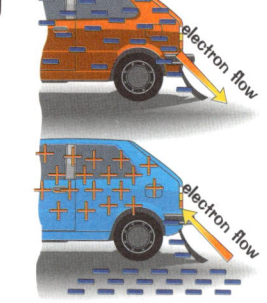

3) Like Charges Repel, Opposite Charges Attract

This is _easy_ and, I'd have thought, _kind of obvious_.
Two things with _opposite_ electric charges are _attracted_ to each other.
Two things with the _same_ electric charge will _repel_ each other.
These forces get _weaker_ the _further apart_ the two things are.

4) As Charge Builds Up, So Does the Voltage — Causing Sparks

The greater the _CHARGE_ on an _isolated_ object, the greater the _VOLTAGE_ between it and the Earth. If the voltage gets _big enough_ there's a _spark_ which _jumps_ across the gap. High voltage cables can be _dangerous_ for this reason. Big sparks have been known to _leap_ from _overhead cables_ to earth. But not often.

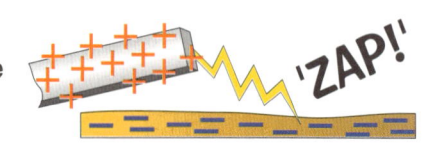

Phew — it's enough to make your hair stand on end...

The way to tackle this page is to first _learn the four headings_ till you can _scribble them all down_. Then learn the details for each one, and keep practising by _covering the page_ and scribbling down each heading with as many details as you can remember for each one. Just _keep trying_...

Static Electricity — Examples

Electric Charge

They like asking you to give _quite detailed examples_ in Exams. Make sure you _learn all these details_.

Static Electricity Being Helpful:

1) Inkjet Printer:

1) Tiny droplets of ink are forced out of a _fine nozzle_, making them _electrically charged_.
2) The droplets are _deflected_ as they pass between two metal plates. A _voltage_ is applied to the plates — one is _negative_ and the other is _positive_.
3) The droplets are _attracted_ to the plate of the _same_ charge and _repelled_ from the plate with the _opposite_ charge.
4) The _size_ and _direction_ of the voltage across each plate changes so each droplet is deflected to hit a _different place_ on the paper.
5) Loads of tiny dots make up your printout. Clever.

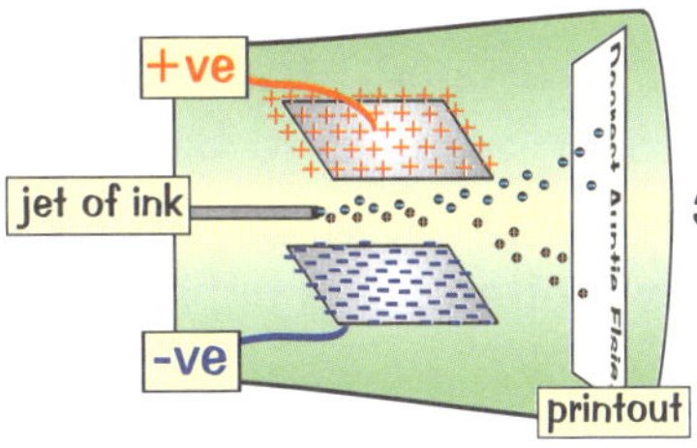

2) Photocopier:

1) The _metal plate_ is electrically charged. An image of what you're copying is projected onto it.
2) Whiter bits of the thing you're copying make _light_ fall on the plate and the charge _leaks away_.
3) The charged bits attract _black powder_, which is transferred onto paper.
4) The paper is _heated_ so the powder sticks.
5) Voilà, a photocopy of your piece of paper (or whatever else you've shoved in there).

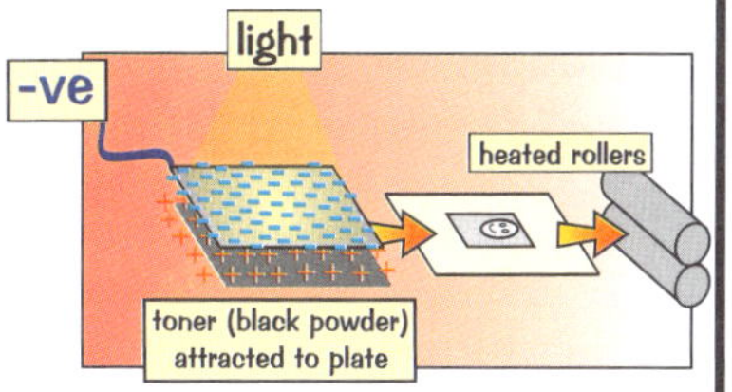

3) Spray Painting and Dust Removal in Chimneys...
But photocopiers and inkjet printers are what they _really_ want you to learn.

Static Electricity Being a Little Joker:

1) Car Shocks
Air rushing past your car can give it a +ve charge. When you get out and touch the door it gives you a real buzz — in the Exam make sure you say "electrons flow from earth, through you, to neutralise the +ve charge on the car. Some cars have conducting rubber strips which hang down behind the car. This gives a safe discharge to earth, but spoils all the fun.

2) Clothing Crackles
When synthetic clothes are dragged over each other (like in a tumble drier) or over your head, electrons get scraped off, leaving static charges on both parts, and that leads to the inevitable — attraction (they stick together) and little sparks / shocks as the charges rearrange themselves.

Static Electricity Playing at Terrorist:

1) Lightning
Rain droplets fall to Earth with positive charge. This creates a huge voltage and a big spark.

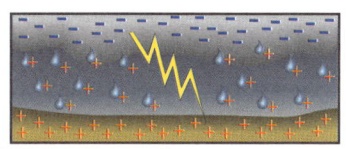

2) Grain Shoots, Paper Rollers and The Fuel Filling Nightmare:

1) As fuel flows out of a filler pipe, or paper drags over rollers, or grain shoots out of pipes, then static can build up.
2) This can easily lead to a spark and in dusty or fumey places — BOOM!
3) The solution: make the nozzles or rollers out of metal so that the charge is conducted away, instead of building up.
4) It's also good to have earthing straps between the fuel tank and the fuel pipe.

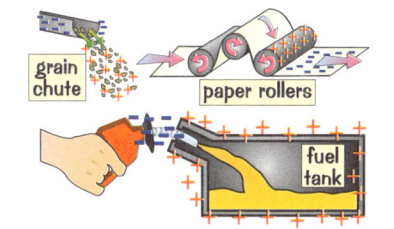

Static Electricity — learn the shocking truth...

You _really_ need to learn those two big examples at the top. The specification mentions photocopiers and inkjet printers so there's bound to be a question. Good grief, it's almost relevant to real life too. Learn the numbered points and keep scribbling them down to check.

Section One — Electricity   AQA Syllabus

Electrolysis

Electric Charge

In the two examples below the charges are *free* to move in the substance in which they are formed.

In Metals the Current is Carried by Electrons

1) Electric current will only flow if there are *charges* which can *move freely*.
2) Metals contain a *"sea" of free electrons* (which are negatively charged) and which *flow* throughout the metal.
3) This is what allows *electric current* to flow so well in *all* metals.

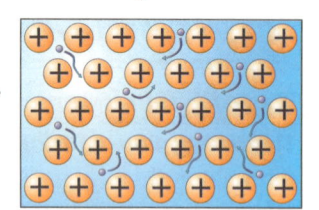

In Electrolytes, Current is Carried by Both +ve and −ve Charges

Copper Chloride will *not conduct* electricity in its normal state as a *solid* because there are *no free charges* moving around. In order for Copper Chloride to conduct electricity then charges need to be able to *flow freely* in the substance, this is achieved by either dissolving the substance in water or heating it until it is molten. The substance then becomes an *electrolyte*:

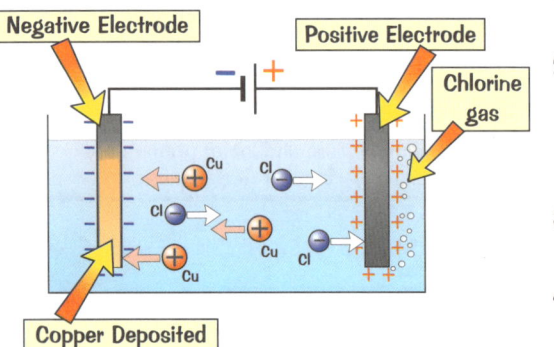

1) *Electrolytes* are liquids which contain charges which can *move freely*.
2) When a voltage is applied across the liquid the *positive* charges move towards the *−ve* electrode, and the *negative* charges move towards the *+ve* electrode. This is an *electric current*.
3) This process is called *electrolysis*. The substance is now conducting electricity.
4) Substances form at the electrodes during this process, for example in copper chloride solution, *Copper* forms at the *negative electrode*.

This build up of matter *increases* when:
1) The current *increases*.
2) The current flows for a *longer period*.

Don't forget: *more current means more charge* — which gives us this important rule:

The amount of matter deposited is proportional to the amount of charge that has flowed.

Example: 1200 coulombs of charge flowing through copper chloride solution produces 0.5g of copper at the negative electrode. How much copper is produced by:
  a) A 1 amp current flowing for 10 minutes?
  b) A 4 amp current flowing for 5 minutes?

Answer:
a) First find the amount of charge that has flowed in 10 minutes: charge = current × time ($Q = I \times t$). Q = 1 × 600 = *600 coulombs*.
   This is *half* the original charge that flowed and so the matter deposited is half the original amount, i.e. *0.25g*.
b) Q = 4 × 300 = *1200 coulombs*.
   This is the *same* amount of charge that originally flowed so *0.5g* of copper forms at the negative electrode.

Electrolysis — time to recharge those batteries...

A bit of higher learning here, but two simple mini-essays to rewrite with all those lovely important points to remember. Learn the details then go for a quick walk, come back and write it all down. Check back to see what you missed, then try again.

Revision Summary For Section One

Electricity and magnetism. What fun. This is definitely Physics at its most grisly. The big problem with Physics in general is that usually there's nothing to "see". You're told that there's a current flowing or a magnetic field lurking, but there's nothing you can actually see with your eyes. That's what makes it so difficult. To get to grips with Physics you have to get used to learning about things which you can't see. Try these questions and see how well you're doing.

1) Describe what current, voltage and resistance are.
2) Sketch out the standard test circuit with all the details. Describe how it's used.
3) Sketch the four standard V-I graphs and explain their shapes. How do you get R from them?
4) Scribble down 17 circuit symbols that you know, with their names of course.
5) Write down two facts about: a) variable resistor b) diode c) LDR d) thermistor.
6) Sketch a typical series circuit and say why it is a series circuit, not a parallel one.
7) State five rules about the current, voltage and resistance in a series circuit.
8) Give examples of lights wired in series and wired in parallel and explain the main differences.
9) Sketch a typical parallel circuit, showing voltmeter and ammeter positions.
10) State five rules about the current, voltage and resistance in a parallel circuit.
11) Draw a circuit diagram of part of a car's electrics, and explain why they are in parallel.
12) What are the four types of energy that electricity can easily be converted into?
13) Sketch a view of a circuit to explain the formula "E=QV". Which dull definitions go with it?
14) Write down six electrical hazards in the home.
15) Sketch a properly wired plug. Explain how fuses work.
16) Explain fully how earthing works.
17) Sketch an electricity meter and explain exactly what the number on it represents.
18) What's a kilowatt-hour? What are the two easy formulae for finding the cost of electricity?
19) What carries current in metals? What's "conventional current" and what's the problem?
20) What is static electricity? What is nearly always the cause of it building up?
21) Which particles move when static builds up, and which ones don't?
22) Give *an* example of static being: a) helpful   b) a little joker   c) terrorist.
23) Draw a diagram of electrolysis in action and explain how it works.

Section One — Electricity
AQA Syllabus

Forces and Motion

Mass, Weight and Gravity

Representing and Measuring Motion

Gravity is the Force of Attraction Between All Masses

Gravity attracts *all* masses, but you only notice it when one of the masses is *really really big*, e.g. a planet. Anything near a planet or star is *attracted* to it *very strongly*. This has *three* important effects:

1) It makes all things *accelerate* towards the *ground* (all with the *same* acceleration, *g*, which = $10m/s^2$ on Earth).
2) It gives everything a *weight*.
3) It keeps *planets*, *moons* and *satellites* in their *orbits*. The orbit is a *balance* between the *forward* motion of the object and the force of gravity pulling it *inwards*.

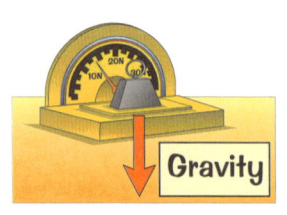

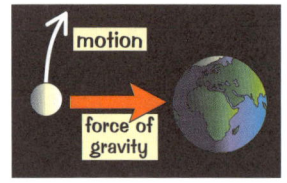

Weight and Mass are Not the Same

To understand this you must *learn all these facts* about *mass and weight*.

1) MASS is the AMOUNT OF MATTER in an object.
   For any given object this will have the same value ANYWHERE in the Universe.
2) WEIGHT is caused by the *pull* of gravity. In most questions the *weight* of an object is just the *force* of gravity pulling it towards the centre of the *Earth*.
3) An object has the *same* mass whether it's on *Earth* or on the *Moon* — but its *weight* will be *different*. A 1 kg mass will *weigh LESS* on the Moon (1.6N) than it does on *Earth* (10N), simply because the *force* of gravity pulling on it is *less*.
4) Weight is a *force* measured in *newtons*. It must be measured using a *spring* balance or *newton meter*. MASS is NOT a force. It's measured in *kilograms* with a *mass* balance (never a spring balance).

5) One very fancy definition of a *newton*. You need to know it.

ONE NEWTON is the force needed to give a MASS OF 1 kg an ACCELERATION OF $1m/s^2$

The Very Important Formula relating Mass, Weight and Gravity

$$W = m \times g$$

(Weight = mass × g)

1) Remember, weight and mass are NOT the same. Mass is in *kg*, weight is in *newtons*.
2) The letter "g" represents the *strength* of the gravity and its value is *different* for *different planets*. On Earth g = 10 N/kg. On the Moon, where the gravity is weaker, g is just 1.6 N/kg.
3) This formula is *hideously easy* to use:

EXAMPLE: What is the weight, in newtons, of a 5kg mass, both on Earth and on the Moon?

Answer: "W = m × g". On Earth: W = 5 × 10 = **50N** (The weight of the 5kg mass is 50N)
On the Moon: W = 5 × 1.6 = **8N** (The weight of the 5kg mass is 8N)

See what I mean. Hideously easy — as long as you've learnt what all the letters mean.

Learn about gravity NOW — no point in "weighting" around...

Very often, the only way to "*understand*" something is to *learn all the facts about it*. That's certainly true here. "Understanding" the difference between mass and weight is no more than learning all those facts about them. When you've learnt all those facts, you'll understand it.

AQA Syllabus — *Section Two — Forces and Motion*

Velocity and Acceleration

Forces and Acceleration

Speed and Velocity are Both just: HOW FAST YOU'RE GOING

Speed and velocity are both measured in m/s (or km/h or mph). They both simply say how fast you're going, but there's a subtle difference between them which you need to know:

SPEED is just **HOW FAST** you're going (e.g. 30mph or 20m/s) with no regard to the direction.
VELOCITY however must **ALSO** have the **DIRECTION** specified, e.g. 30mph *north* or 20m/s, 060°

Seems kinda fussy I know, but they expect you to remember that distinction, so there you go.

Speed, Distance and Time — the Formula:

$$\text{Speed} = \frac{\text{Distance}}{\text{Time}}$$

$$\frac{d}{s \times t}$$

You really ought to get *pretty slick* with this *very easy formula*.
As usual the *formula triangle* version makes it all a bit of a *breeze*.
You just need to try and think up some interesting word for remembering the *order* of the *letters* in the triangle, s^{d}t. Errm... sedit, perhaps... well, you think up your own.

EXAMPLE: A cat skulks 20m in 35s. Find a) its speed   b) how long it takes to skulk 75m.
ANSWER: Using the formula triangle: a) s = d/t = 20/35 = <u>0.57m/s</u>
                                           b) t = d/s = 75/0.57 = 131s = <u>2mins 11sec</u>

A lot of the time we tend to use the words "speed" and "velocity" interchangeably.
For example to calculate velocity you'd just use the above formula for speed instead.

Acceleration is How Quickly You're Speeding Up

Acceleration is definitely *NOT* the same as *velocity* or *speed*.
   Every time you read or write the word *acceleration*, remind yourself: "*acceleration* is *COMPLETELY DIFFERENT* from *velocity*. Acceleration is how *quickly* the velocity is *changing*."
Velocity is a simple idea. Acceleration is altogether more *subtle*, which is why it's *confusing*.

Acceleration — The Formula:

$$\text{Acceleration} = \frac{\text{Change in Velocity}}{\text{Time Taken}}$$

$$\frac{\Delta V}{a \times t}$$

Well, it's *just another formula*. Just like all the others. Three things in a *formula triangle*.
Mind you, there are *two* tricky things with this one. First there's the "ΔV", which means working out the "*change in velocity*", as shown in the example below, rather than just putting a *simple value* for speed or velocity in. Secondly there's the *units* of acceleration which are m/s^2.
Not m/s, which is *velocity*, but m/s^2. Got it? No? Let's try once more: *Not m/s, but m/s^2*.

EXAMPLE: A skulking cat accelerates from 2m/s to 6m/s in 5.6s. Find its acceleration.
ANSWER: Using the formula triangle: a = ΔV/t = (6 - 2) / 5.6 = 4 ÷ 5.6 = <u>0.71 m/s^2</u>
         All pretty basic stuff I'd say.

Velocity and Acceleration — learn the difference...

It's true — some people don't realise that velocity and acceleration are totally different things. Hard to believe I know — all part of the great mystery and tragedy of life I suppose.
Anyway. Learn the definitions and the formulae, *cover the page* and *scribble it all down again*.

Section Two — Forces and Motion   AQA Syllabus

D-T and V-T Graphs

Forces and Acceleration

Make sure you learn all these details real good. Make sure you can *distinguish* between the two, too.

Distance-Time Graphs

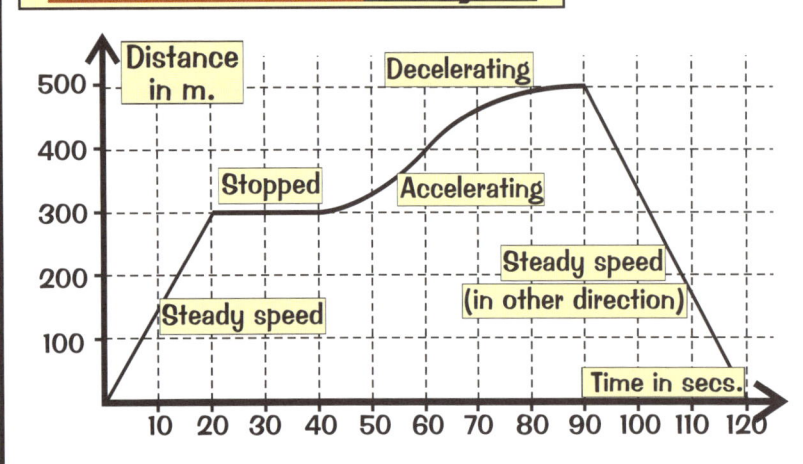

Very Important Notes:

1) **GRADIENT = SPEED**.
2) *Flat* sections are where it's *stopped*.
3) The *steeper* the graph, the *faster* it's going.
4) *Downhill* sections mean it's *coming back* toward its starting point.
5) *Curves* represent *acceleration* or deceleration.
6) A *steepening* curve means it's *speeding up* (increasing gradient).
7) A *levelling off* curve means it's *slowing down* (decreasing gradient).

Calculating Speed from a Distance-Time Graph — it's just the Gradient

For example the *speed* of the *return* section of the graph is:

Speed = gradient = vertical/horizontal = 500/30 = 16.7 m/s

Don't forget that you have to use the *scales* of the axes to work out the gradient. *Don't* measure in *cm*!

Velocity-Time Graphs

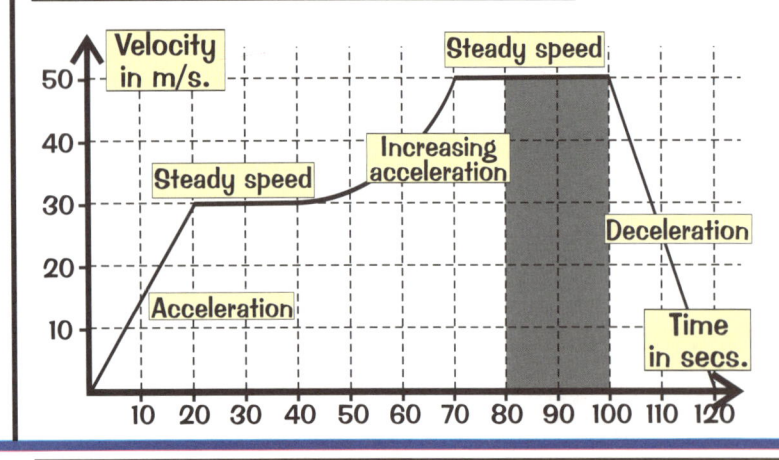

Very Important Notes:

1) **GRADIENT = ACCELERATION**.
2) *Flat* sections represent *steady* speed.
3) The *steeper* the graph, the *greater* the *acceleration* or deceleration.
4) *Uphill* sections (/) are *acceleration*.
5) *Downhill* sections (\) — *deceleration*.
6) The *area* under any section of the graph (or all of it) is equal to the *distance* travelled in that *time* interval.
7) A *curve* means *changing acceleration*.

Calculating Acceleration, Speed and Distance from a Velocity-time Graph

1) The *ACCELERATION* represented by the *first section* of the graph is:

Acceleration = gradient = vertical/horizontal = 30/20 = 1.5 m/s²

2) The *SPEED* at any point is simply found by *reading the value* off the *speed axis*.
3) The *DISTANCE TRAVELLED* in any time interval is equal to the *area*. For example, the distance travelled between t=80 and t=100 is equal to the *shaded area* which is equal to *1000m*.

Understanding speed and stuff — it can be an uphill struggle...

The tricky thing about these two kinds of graph is that they can look pretty much the same but represent totally different kinds of motion. If you want to be able to do them (in the Exam) then there's no substitute for simply *learning all the numbered points* for both types. Enjoy.

The Three Laws of Motion

Forces and Acceleration

Around about the time of the Great Plague in the 1660s, a chap called _Isaac Newton_ worked out _The Three Laws of Motion_. At first they might seem kind of obscure or irrelevant, but to be perfectly blunt, if you can't understand these _three simple laws_ then you'll never fully understand _forces and motion_:

First Law — Balanced Forces mean No Change in Velocity

So long as the forces on an object are all _BALANCED_, then it'll just _STAY STILL_, or else if it's already moving it'll just carry on at the _SAME VELOCITY_ — so long as the forces are all _BALANCED_.

1) When a train or car or bus or anything else is _moving_ at a _constant velocity_ then the _forces_ on it must all be _BALANCED_.
2) Never let yourself entertain the _ridiculous idea_ that things need a constant overall force to _keep_ them moving — NO NO NO NO NO NO!
3) To keep going at a _steady speed_, there must be _ZERO RESULTANT FORCE_ — and don't you forget it.

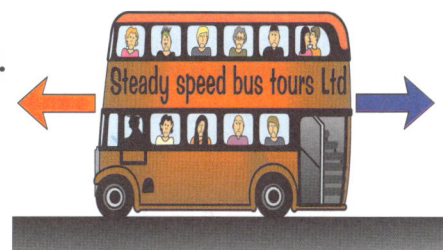

Second Law — A Resultant Force means Acceleration

If there is an _UNBALANCED FORCE_, then the object will _ACCELERATE_ in that direction.

1) An _unbalanced_ force will always produce _acceleration_ (or deceleration).
2) This "_acceleration_" can take _FIVE_ different forms:
   Starting, _stopping_, _speeding up_, _slowing down_ and _changing direction_.
3) On a force diagram, the _arrows_ will be _unequal_:

Don't ever say: "If something's moving there must be an overall resultant force acting on it".

Not so. If there's an _overall_ force it will always _accelerate_. You get _steady_ speed from _balanced_ forces. I wonder how many times I need to say that same thing before you remember it?

Three Points Which Should Be Obvious:

1) The bigger the _force_, the _GREATER_ the _acceleration_ or _deceleration_.
2) The bigger the _mass_ the _SMALLER the acceleration_.
3) To get a _big_ mass to accelerate _as fast_ as a _small_ mass it needs a _bigger_ force.
   Just think about pushing _heavy_ trolleys and it should all seem _fairly obvious_, I would hope.

The Overall Unbalanced Force is often called The Resultant Force

Any _resultant force_ will produce _acceleration_ and this is the _formula_ for it:

$$F = ma \quad \text{or} \quad a = F/m$$

m = mass, a = acceleration   F is always the _RESULTANT FORCE_

Section Two — Forces and Motion   AQA Syllabus

The Three Laws of Motion

Forces and Acceleration

Calculations using F = ma — An Example

Q) What force is needed to accelerate a mass of *12kg* at *5m/s²* ?
ANS. The question is asking for *force*
— so you need a formula with "*F = something-or-other*".
Since they also give you values for *mass* and *acceleration*, the formula "*F = ma*" really should be a *pretty obvious choice*, surely.
So just *stick* in the numbers they give you where the letters are:
m = 12, *a = 5*, so "*F = ma*" gives F = 12 × 5 = *60N* (It's *newtons* because force always is)
(Notice that you don't really need to *fully understand* what's going on — you just need to know *how to use formulae*.)

The Third Law — Reaction Forces

If object A EXERTS A FORCE on object B then object B exerts THE EXACT OPPOSITE FORCE on object A

1) That means if you *push* against a wall, the wall will *push back* against you, *just as hard*.

2) And as soon as you *stop* pushing, *so does the wall*. Kinda clever really.

3) If you think about it, there must be an *opposing force* when you lean against a wall — otherwise you (and the wall) would *fall over*.

4) If you *pull* a cart, whatever force *you exert* on the rope, the rope exerts the *exact opposite* pull on *you*.

5) If you put a book on a table, the *weight* of the book acts *downwards* on the table, — and the table exerts an *equal and opposite* force *upwards* on the book.

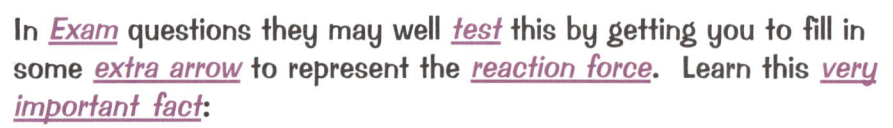

6) If you support a book on your *hand*, the book exerts its *weight* downwards on you, and you provide an *upwards* force on the book and it all stays nicely *in balance*.

In *Exam* questions they may well *test* this by getting you to fill in some *extra arrow* to represent the *reaction force*. Learn this *very important fact*:

Whenever an object is on a horizontal SURFACE, there'll always be a REACTION FORCE pushing UPWARDS, supporting the object. The total REACTION FORCE will be EQUAL AND OPPOSITE to the weight.

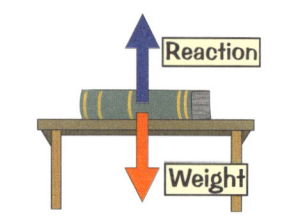

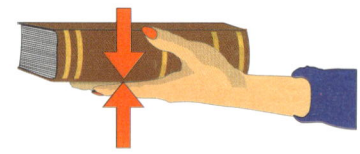

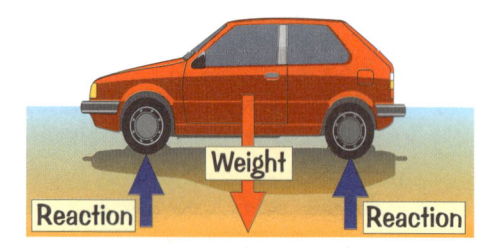

Hey, did you know — an unbalanced force causes ac...

Good old Isaac. Those three laws of motion are pretty inspirational don't you think? No? Oh. Well you could do with learning them anyway, because in this topic there are hardly any nice easy facts that'll help — in the end there's *no substitute* for fully understanding *The Three Laws*.

AQA Syllabus   *Section Two — Forces and Motion*

Force Diagrams

Forces and Acceleration

A _force_ is simply a _push_ or a _pull_. There are only _six_ different forces for you to know about:

1) GRAVITY or WEIGHT always acting straight _downwards_.
2) REACTION FORCE from a _surface_, usually acting _straight upwards_.
3) THRUST or PUSH or PULL due to an engine or rocket _speeding something up_.
4) DRAG or AIR RESISTANCE or FRICTION which is _slowing the thing down_.
5) LIFT due to an _aeroplane wing_.
6) TENSION in a _rope_ or _cable_.

And there are basically only FIVE DIFFERENT FORCE DIAGRAMS you can get:

1) Stationary Object — All Forces in Balance

1) The force of GRAVITY (or weight) is acting _downwards_.
2) This causes a REACTION FORCE from the surface _pushing_ the object _back up_.
3) This is the _only way_ it can be in BALANCE.
4) _Without_ a reaction force, it would accelerate _downwards_ due to the pull of gravity.
5) The two HORIZONTAL forces must be _equal and opposite_ otherwise the object will accelerate _sideways_.

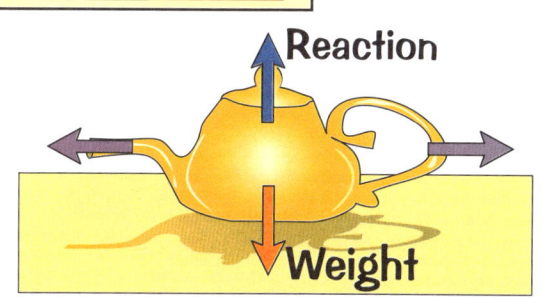

2) Steady Horizontal Velocity — All Forces in Balance!

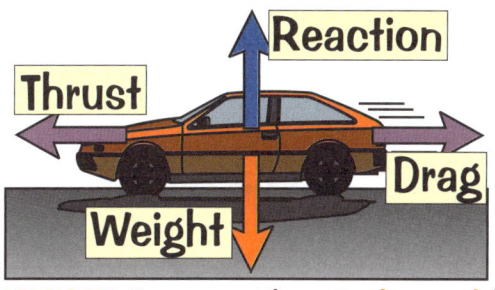

3) Steady Vertical Velocity — All Forces in Balance!

TAKE NOTE! To move with a _steady speed_ the forces must be in BALANCE. If there is an _unbalanced force_ then you get ACCELERATION, not steady speed. That's _rrrreal important_ so don't forget it.

4) Horizontal Acceleration — Unbalanced Forces

1) You only get _acceleration_ with an overall _resultant_ (unbalanced) _force_.
2) The _bigger_ this _unbalanced force_, the _greater_ the _acceleration_.

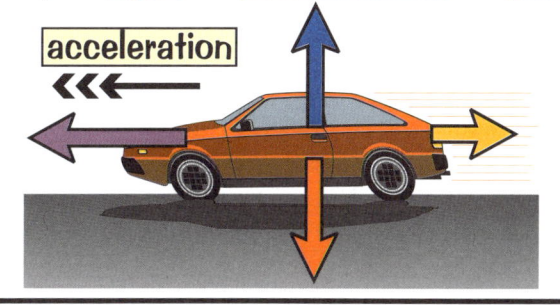

Note that the forces in the _other direction_ are still _balanced_.

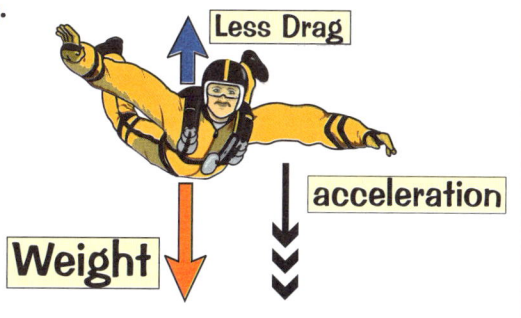

5) Vertical Acceleration — Unbalanced Forces

Revise Force Diagrams — but don't become unbalanced...

Make sure you learn those five different force diagrams. You'll almost certainly get one of them in your Exam. All you really need to remember is how the relative sizes of the arrows relate to the type of motion. It's pretty simple so long as you make the effort to _learn it_. So _scribble_...

Section Two — Forces and Motion   AQA Syllabus

Terminal Velocity
Forces and Acceleration

Resultant Force is Real Important — Especially for "F = ma"

The notion of RESULTANT FORCE is a real important one for you to get your head round. It's not especially tricky, it's just that it seems to get kind of ignored.

In most real situations there are at least two forces acting on an object along any direction. The overall effect of these forces will decide the motion of the object — whether it will accelerate, decelerate or stay at a steady speed. The "overall effect" is found by just adding or subtracting the forces which point along the same direction. The overall force you get is called the RESULTANT FORCE.

And when you use the formula "F = ma", F must always be the RESULTANT FORCE.

EXAMPLE: A car of mass of 1750kg has an engine which provides a driving force of 5,200N.
At 70mph the drag force acting on the car is 5,150N.
Find its acceleration a) when first setting off from rest b) at 70mph.

ANSWER: 1) First draw a force diagram for both cases (no need to show the vertical forces):

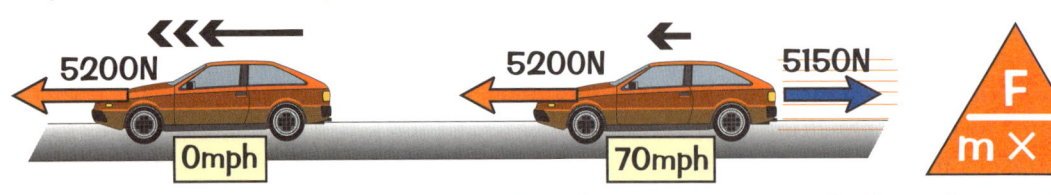

2) Work out the resultant force in each case, and apply "F = ma" using the formula triangle:

Resultant force = 5,200N
a = F/m = 5,200 ÷ 1750 = **3.0 m/s²**

Resultant force = 5,200 − 5,150 = 50N
a = F/m = 50 ÷ 1750 = **0.03 m/s²**

Cars and Free-Fallers all Reach a Terminal Velocity

When cars and free-falling objects first set off they have much more force accelerating them than resistance slowing them down. As the speed increases the resistance builds up. This gradually reduces the acceleration until eventually the resistance force is equal to the accelerating force and then it won't be able to accelerate any more. It will have reached its maximum speed or TERMINAL VELOCITY.

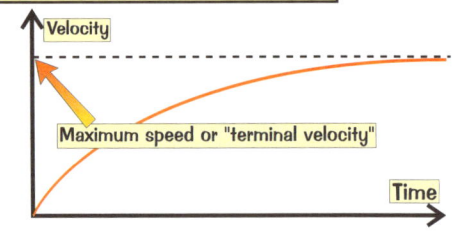

The Terminal Velocity of Falling Objects depends on their Shape and Area

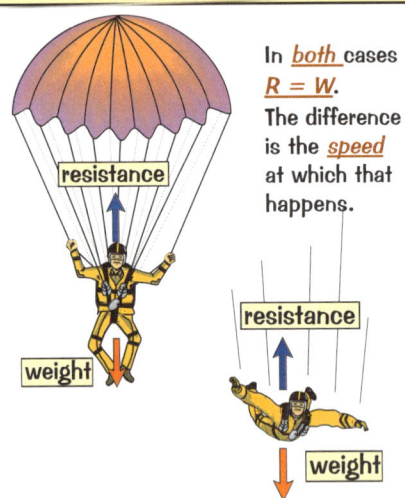

In both cases R = W.
The difference is the speed at which that happens.

The accelerating force acting on all falling objects is GRAVITY and it would make them all fall at the same rate, if it wasn't for air resistance.
To prove this, on the Moon, where there's no air, hamsters and feathers dropped simultaneously will hit the ground together.
However, on Earth, air resistance causes things to fall at different speeds, and the terminal velocity of any object is determined by its drag in comparison to the weight of it. The drag depends on its shape and area.

The most important example is the human skydiver. Without his parachute open he has quite a small area and a force of "W=mg" pulling him down. He reaches a terminal velocity of about 120mph.
But with the parachute open, there's much more air resistance (at any given speed) and still only the same force "W=mg" pulling him down. This means his terminal velocity comes right down to about 15mph, which is a safe speed to hit the ground at.

Learning about Air resistance — it can be a real drag...

It looks like mini-essay time to me. There's a lot of details swirling around here, so definitely the best way of checking how much you know is to scribble down a mini-essay for each of the three sections. Then check back and see what you missed. Then try again. And keep trying.

AQA Syllabus   Section Two — Forces and Motion

Friction

Frictional Forces and Non-Uniform Motion

1) Friction is Always There to Slow things Down

1) If an object has no force propelling it along it will always slow down and stop because of friction.
2) Friction always acts in the opposite direction to movement.
3) To travel at a steady speed, the driving force needs to balance the frictional forces.
4) Friction occurs in THREE main ways:

a) FRICTION BETWEEN SOLID SURFACES WHICH ARE GRIPPING

For example between tyres and the road. There's always a limit as to how far two surfaces can grip each other, and if you demand more force of friction than they can manage, then they start to slide past each other instead. i.e. if you try to brake too hard, you'll SKID.

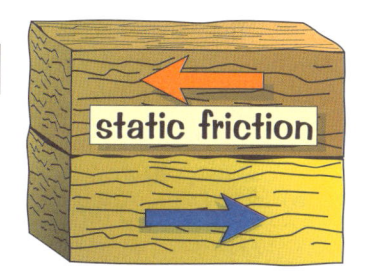

static friction

b) FRICTION BETWEEN SOLID SURFACES WHICH ARE SLIDING PAST EACH OTHER

For example between brake pads and brake discs. There's just as much force of friction here as between the tyres and the road. In fact in the end, if you brake hard enough the friction here becomes greater than at the tyres, and then the wheel skids.

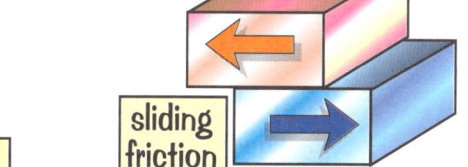

sliding friction

c) RESISTANCE OR "DRAG" FROM FLUIDS (AIR OR LIQUID)

The most important factor by far in reducing drag in fluids is keeping the shape of the object streamlined, like fish bodies or boat hulls or bird wings/bodies. The opposite extreme is a parachute which is about as high drag as you can get — which is, of course, the whole idea.

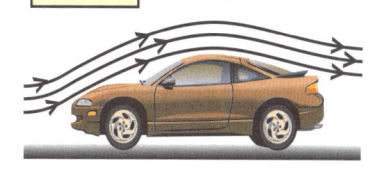

2) Friction Always Increases as the Speed Increases

A car has much more friction to work against when travelling at 60mph compared to 30mph. So at 60mph the engine has to work much harder just to maintain a steady speed.
It therefore uses more petrol than it would going just as far at 30mph.

3) But We Also Need Friction to Move and to Stop!

It's easy to think of friction as generally a nuisance because we always seem to be working against it, but don't forget that without it we wouldn't be able to walk or run or race off the line at the traffic lights or screech round corners or go sky-diving or do just about anything exciting or interesting. It also holds nuts and bolts together. Life without friction — that would be a drag.

4) Friction Causes Wear and Heating

1) Friction always acts between surfaces that are sliding over each other. Machinery has lots of surfaces doing that.
2) Friction always produces heat and wearing of the surfaces.
3) Lubricants are used to keep the friction as low as possible and thus reduce wear.

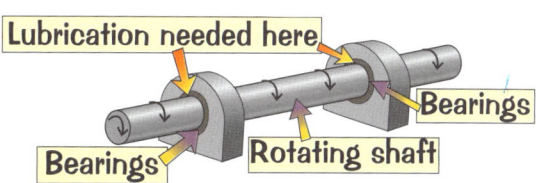

Learn about friction — just don't let it wear you down...

I would never have thought there was so much to say about friction. Nevertheless, there it all is, all mentioned in the AQA syllabus, and all very likely to come up in your Exam. Ignore it at your peril. Learn the seven main headings, then the stuff, then cover the page and away you go.

Section Two — Forces and Motion   *AQA Syllabus*

Stopping Distances for Cars

Frictional Forces and Non-Uniform Motion

They're pretty keen on this for Exam questions, so make sure you *learn it properly*.

The Many Factors Which Affect Your Total Stopping Distance

The distance it takes to stop a car is divided into the THINKING DISTANCE and the BRAKING DISTANCE.

1) Thinking Distance

"The distance the car travels in the split-second between a hazard appearing and the driver applying the brakes".

The figures below for typical stopping distances are from the Highway code. It's frightening to see just how far it takes to stop when you're going at 70mph.

It's affected by THREE MAIN FACTORS:

a) *How FAST you're going* — obviously. Whatever your reaction time, the *faster* you're going, the *further* you'll go.

b) *How DOPEY you are* — This is affected by *tiredness*, *drugs*, *alcohol*, *old-age*, and a *careless* blasé attitude.

c) *How BAD the VISIBILITY is* — lashing rain and oncoming lights, etc. make *hazards* harder to spot.

30 mph	50 mph	70 mph
9m	15m	21m
14m	38m	75m
6 car lengths	13 car lengths	24 car lengths

2) Braking Distance

"The distance the car travels during its deceleration whilst the brakes are being applied".

It's affected by FOUR MAIN FACTORS:

a) *How FAST you're going* — obviously. The *faster* you're going the *further* it takes to stop (see below).

b) *How HEAVILY LOADED the vehicle is* — with the *same* brakes, *a heavily-laden* vehicle takes *longer to stop*. A car won't stop as quick when it's full of people and luggage and towing a caravan.

c) *How good your BRAKES are* — all brakes must be checked and maintained *regularly*. Worn or faulty brakes will let you down *catastrophically* just when you need them the *most*, i.e. in an *emergency*.

d) *How good the GRIP is* — this depends on THREE THINGS:
1) *road surface*, 2) *weather* conditions, 3) *tyres*.

Leaves and diesel spills and muck on t'road are *serious hazards* because they're *unexpected*. *Wet* or *icy roads* are always much more *slippy* than dry roads, but often you only discover this when you try to *brake* hard! Tyres should have a minimum *tread depth* of *1.6mm*. This is essential for getting rid of the *water* in wet conditions. Without *tread*, a tyre will simply *ride* on a *layer of water* and skid *very easily*. This is called "*aquaplaning*" and isn't nearly as cool as it sounds.

Stopping Distances Increase Alarmingly with Extra Speed

— Mainly Because of the v^2 bit in KE=½mv²

To stop a car, the *kinetic energy*, ½mv², has to be *converted to heat energy* at the *brakes and tyres*: If you *double the speed*, you double the value of *v*, but the v^2 means that the *KE* is then increased by a factor of *four*. This means that you need *4 times* the *distance* to stop when applying the *maximum* possible braking force.

Muck on t'road, eh — by gum, it's grim up North...

They mention this specifically in the syllabus and are very likely to test you on it since it involves safety. Learn all the details and write yourself a *mini-essay* to see how much you *really know*.

AQA Syllabus — Section Two — Forces and Motion

Revision Summary for Section Two

More jolly questions which I know you're going to really enjoy. There are lots of bits and bobs on forces, motion and pressure which you definitely need to know. Some bits are certainly quite tricky to understand, but there's also loads of straightforward stuff which just need to be learnt, ready for instant regurgitation in the Exam. You have to practise these questions over and over and over again, until you can answer them all really easily — phew, such jolly fun.

1) What is gravity? List the three main effects that gravity produces.
2) Explain the difference between mass and weight. What units are they measured in?
3) What's the formula for weight? Illustrate it with a worked example of your own.
4) What's the difference between speed and velocity? Give an example of each.
5) Write down the formula for working out speed. Find the speed of a partly chewed mouse which hobbles 3.2m in 35s. Find how far he would get in 25 minutes.
6) What's acceleration? Is it the same thing as speed or velocity? What are its units?
7) Write down the formula for acceleration. What's the acceleration of a soggy pea, flicked from rest to a speed of 14 m/s in 0.4s?
8) Sketch a typical distance-time graph and point out all the important parts of it.
9) Sketch a typical velocity-time graph and point out all the important parts of it.
10) Write down seven important points relating to each of these graphs.
11) Explain how to calculate velocity from a distance-time graph.
12) Explain how to find speed, distance and acceleration from a velocity-time graph.
13) Write down the First Law of Motion. Illustrate with a diagram.
14) Write down the Second Law of Motion. Illustrate with a diagram. What's the formula for it?
15) A force of 30N pushes on a trolley of mass 4kg. What will be its acceleration?
16) What's the mass of a cat which accelerates at 9.8 m/s^2 when acted on by a force of 56N?
17) Write down the Third Law of Motion. Illustrate it with four diagrams.
18) Explain what <u>reaction force</u> is and where it pops up. Is it important to know about it?
19) List the six different kinds of force. Sketch diagrams to illustrate them all.
20) Sketch each of the five standard force diagrams, showing the forces and the type of motion.
21) Explain what "resultant force" is. Illustrate with a diagram. When do you most need it?
22) What is "terminal velocity"? Is it the same thing as maximum speed?
23) What are the two main factors affecting the terminal velocity of a falling object?
24) List the three types of friction with a sketch to illustrate each one.
25) Describe how friction is affected by speed. What 2 effects does friction have on machinery?
26) Is friction at all useful? Describe five problems we would have if there was no friction.
27) What are the two different parts of the overall stopping distance of a car?
28) List the three or four factors which affect each of the two sections of stopping distance.
29) Which formula explains why the stopping distance increases so much? Explain why it does.

Section Two — Forces and Motion   *AQA Syllabus*

Waves

Waves — Basic Principles — *Characteristics of Waves*

Waves are different from anything else. They have various features which *only waves have*:

Amplitude, Wavelength and Frequency

Too many people get these *wrong*. Take careful note:
1) The AMPLITUDE goes from the *middle* line to the *peak*, NOT from a trough to a peak.
2) The WAVELENGTH covers a *full cycle* of the wave, e.g. from *peak to peak*, not just from "two bits that are sort of separated a bit".
3) FREQUENCY is how many *complete waves* there are *per second* (passing a certain point).

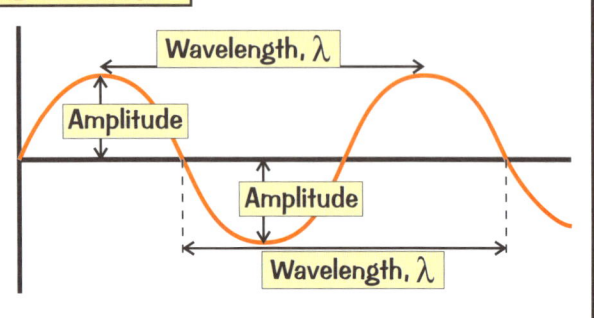

Transverse Waves have Sideways Vibrations

Most waves are TRANSVERSE:
1) *Light* and all other *EM radiation*.
2) *Ripples* on water.
3) *Waves* on *strings*.
4) A *slinky spring* wiggled up and down.

In *TRANSVERSE WAVES* the vibrations are at $90°$ to the *direction of travel* of the wave.

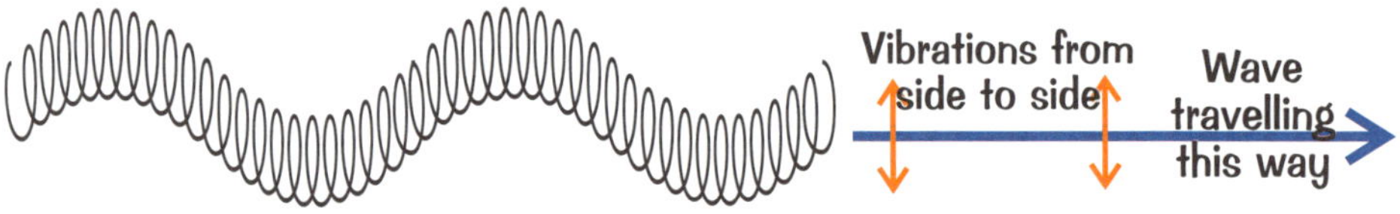

Longitudinal Waves have Vibrations along the Same Line

Examples of longitudinal waves are:
1) *Sound*. It travels as a longitudinal wave through solids, liquids and gases.
2) *Shock waves* e.g. seismic *P-waves*.
3) A *slinky spring* when plucked.
4) *Don't get confused* by CRO displays which shows a *transverse wave* when displaying *sounds*. The real wave is *longitudinal* — the display shows a transverse wave *just so you can see what's going on*.

In *LONGITUDINAL WAVES* the vibrations are *ALONG THE SAME DIRECTION* as the wave is travelling.

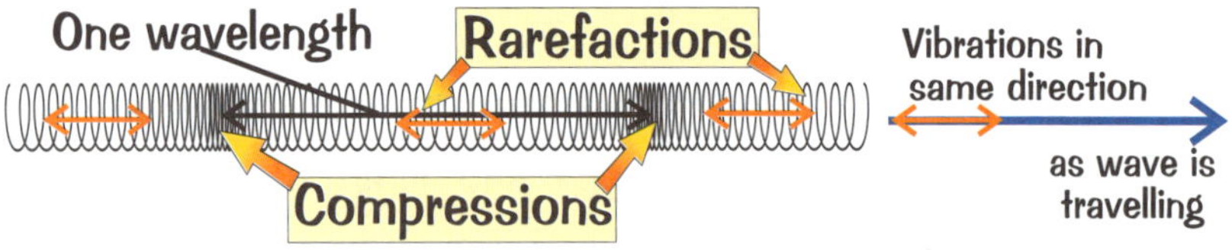

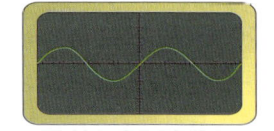

All Waves Carry Energy — Without Transferring Matter

1) *Light*, *infrared*, and *microwaves* all make things *warm up*. *X-rays* and *gamma rays* can cause *ionisation* and *damage* to cells, which also shows that they carry *energy*.
2) *Loud* sounds make things *vibrate or move*. Even the quietest sound moves your *ear drum*.
3) Waves on the sea can *toss big boats around* and can generate *electricity*.

Waves can be REFLECTED and REFRACTED and DIFFRACTED

1) They might test whether or not you realise these are *properties* of waves, so *learn them*.
2) The three words are *confusingly similar* but you MUST learn the *differences* between them.
3) Light and sound are *reflected*, *refracted* and *diffracted* and this shows they travel as waves.

Learn about waves — just get into the vibes, man...

This is all very basic stuff on waves. Five sections with some tasty titbits in each. *Learn* the headings, then the details. Then *cover the page* and see what you can *scribble down*. Then try again until you can remember the whole lot. It's all just *easy marks to be won... or lost*.

AQA Syllabus Section Three — Waves

Reflection

Characteristics of Waves

The Ripple Tank is Really Good for Displaying Waves

Learn all these diagrams showing *reflection of waves*. They could ask you to complete *any one of them* in the Exam. It can be quite a bit *trickier* than you think unless you've *practised* them real well *beforehand*.

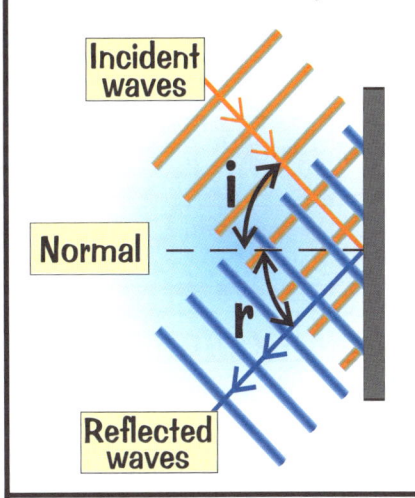

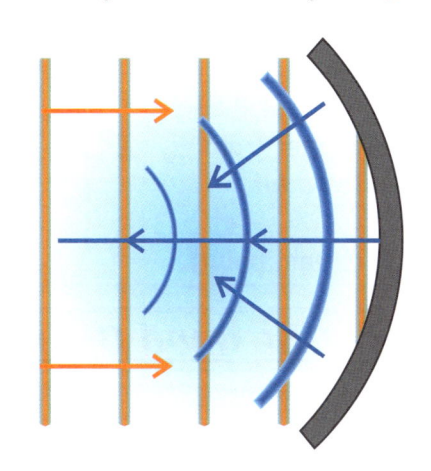

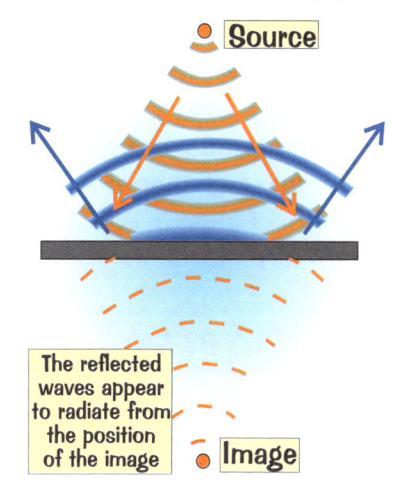

Diagrams: Incident waves hitting a flat barrier with Normal, showing angles i and r, and Reflected waves; plane waves reflecting off a curved barrier converging to a focus; circular waves from a Source reflecting off a flat barrier — "The reflected waves appear to radiate from the position of the image" (Image shown behind barrier).

Reflection of Light

Reflection of light is what allows us to *SEE* objects.
When light reflects from an *even* surface (*smooth and shiny* like a *mirror*) then it's all reflected at the *same angle* and you get a *clear reflection*.
Sound also reflects off *hard surfaces* in the form of *echoes*.
Reflection of light and of sound gives evidence that light and sound travel as waves.
And don't forget, THE LAW OF REFLECTION applies to *every reflected ray*:

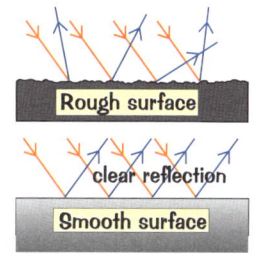

Diagram: Rough surface — scattered reflection; Smooth surface — clear reflection.

Angle of INCIDENCE = Angle of REFLECTION

Reflection In a Plane Mirror — How to Locate The Image

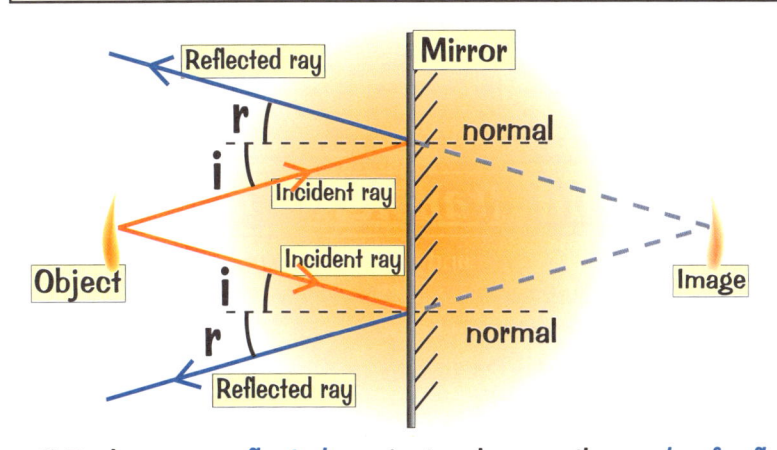

Diagram: Object (flame) in front of Mirror, two incident rays going to the mirror with angles i, reflecting at angles r back to the eye, dotted lines extending behind the mirror locate the Image.

You need to be able to *reproduce* this entire diagram of *how an image is formed* in a PLANE MIRROR.
Learn these *two* important points:

1) The *image* is the *SAME SIZE* as the *object*.
2) It is *AS FAR BEHIND* the mirror as the object is *in front*.

1) To draw *any reflected ray*, just make sure the *angle of reflection*, r, equals the *angle of incidence*, i.
2) Note that these two angles are *ALWAYS* defined between the ray itself and the dotted *NORMAL*.
3) *Don't ever* label them as the angle between the ray and the *surface*. Definitely uncool.

Learn reflection thoroughly — try to look at it from all sides...

First make sure you can draw all those diagrams from memory. Then make sure you've learnt the rest well enough to answer typical meany Exam questions like these: *"Explain why you can see a piece of paper"* *"Why is the image in a plane mirror virtual?"*

Section Three — Waves

Refraction

Characteristics of Waves

1) <u>Refraction</u> is when waves change <u>direction</u> as they enter a <u>different medium</u>.
2) This is caused <u>entirely</u> by the <u>change in speed</u> of the waves.
3) It also causes the <u>wavelength</u> to change, but remember that the <u>frequency</u> does <u>not</u> change.

1) Refraction is Shown by Waves in a Ripple Tank Slowing Down

1) The waves travel <u>slower</u> in <u>shallower water</u>, causing <u>refraction</u> as shown.
2) There's a change in <u>direction</u>, and a change in <u>wavelength</u> but <u>NO change</u> in <u>frequency</u>.

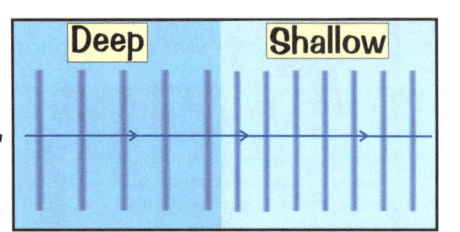

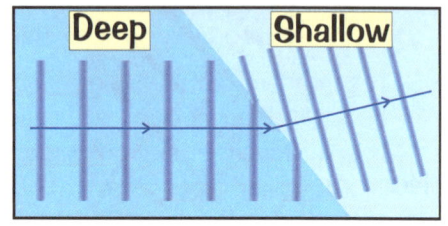

2) Refraction of Light — The Good Old Glass Block Demo

You can't fail to remember the old "<u>ray of light through a rectangular glass block</u>" trick. Make sure you can draw this diagram <u>from memory</u>, with every detail <u>perfect</u>.

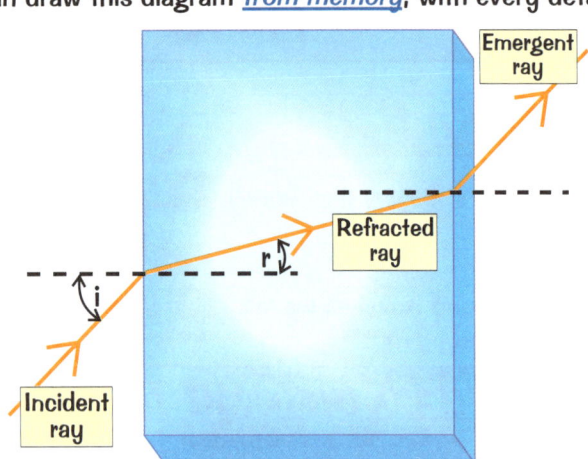

1) <u>Take careful note</u> of the positions of the <u>normals</u> and the <u>exact positions</u> of the angles of <u>incidence</u> and <u>refraction</u> (and note it's the angle of <u>refraction</u> — not <u>reflection</u>).
2) Most important of all remember <u>which way</u> the ray <u>bends</u>.
3) The ray bends <u>towards</u> the normal as it enters the <u>denser medium</u>, and <u>away</u> from the normal as it <u>emerges</u> into the <u>less dense</u> medium.
4) Try to <u>visualise</u> the shape of the <u>wiggle</u> in the diagram — that can be easier than remembering the rule in words.

3) Refraction Is always Caused By the Waves Changing Speed

1) When waves <u>slow down</u> they bend <u>towards</u> the normal.
2) When <u>light</u> enters <u>glass</u> it <u>slows down</u> to about <u>2/3</u> of its normal speed (in air) i.e. it slows down to about 2×10^8 m/s rather than 3×10^8 m/s.
3) When waves hit the boundary <u>along a normal</u>, i.e. at <u>exactly 90°</u>, then there will be <u>no change</u> in direction. That's pretty important to remember, because they often <u>sneak</u> it into a question somewhere. There'll still be a change in <u>speed</u> and <u>wavelength</u>, though.
4) <u>Some</u> light is also <u>reflected</u> when light hits a <u>different medium</u> such as glass.

Normal incidence so no bending

Ray slowed to 2/3 speed wavelength reduced

4) Sound also Refracts But it's Hard to Spot

<u>Sound</u> will also refract (change direction) as it enters <u>different media</u>. However, since sound is always <u>spreading out so much</u>, the change in direction is <u>hard to spot</u> under normal circumstances. But just remember, <u>sound does refract</u>, OK? The fact that sound and light are both refracted gives <u>further evidence</u> that they travel as <u>waves</u>.

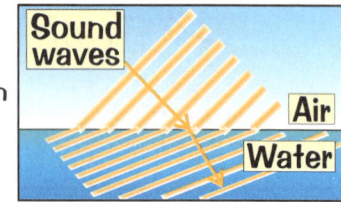

Revise Refraction — but don't let it slow you down...

The first thing you've gotta do is make sure you can spot the difference between the words *refraction* and *reflection*. After that you need to <u>learn all this stuff about refraction</u> — so you know exactly what it is. Make sure you know all those <u>diagrams</u> inside out. <u>Cover and scribble</u>.

AQA Syllabus

Section Three — Waves

Refraction: Two Special Cases

Characteristics of Waves

Dispersion Produces Rainbows

1) *Different colours* of light are *refracted* by *different amounts*.
2) This is because they travel at *slightly different speeds* in any given *medium*.
3) A *prism* can be used to make the different colours of white light emerge at *different angles*.
4) This produces a *spectrum* showing all the colours of the *rainbow*. This effect is called *DISPERSION*.

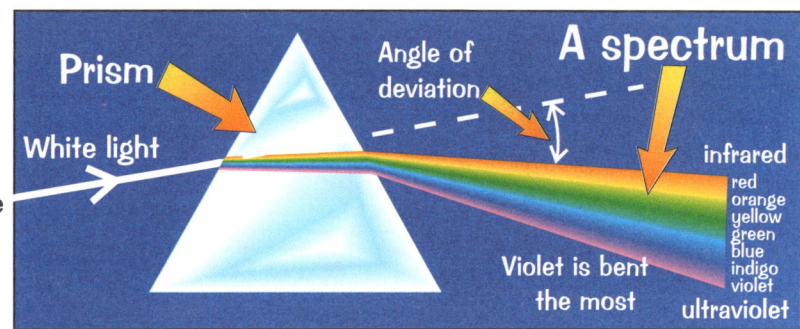

Prism — White light → Angle of deviation → A spectrum (infrared, red, orange, yellow, green, blue, indigo, violet, ultraviolet). Violet is bent the most.

5) You need to know that *red light* is refracted the *least* — and *violet* is refracted the *most*.
6) Also know the *order* of colours in between: Red Orange Yellow Green Blue Indigo Violet
    which is remembered by: Richard Of York Gave Battle In Vain
    They may well test whether you can put them correctly into the diagram.
7) Also learn where *infrared* and *ultraviolet* light would appear if you could detect them.

Total Internal Reflection and the Critical Angle

1) This *only* happens when *light* is *coming out* of something *dense* like *glass* or *water* or *perspex*.
2) If the *angle* is *shallow enough* the ray *won't come out at all*, but it *reflects* back into the glass (or whatever). This is called *total internal reflection* because *ALL* of the light *reflects back in*.
3) You definitely need to learn this set of *THREE DIAGRAMS* which show the three conditions:

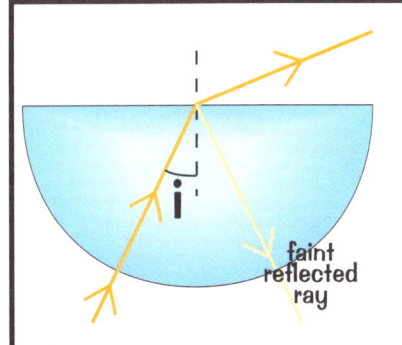

Angle of Incidence LESS than the Critical Angle.
Most of the light *passes through* into the air but a *little* bit of it is *internally reflected*.

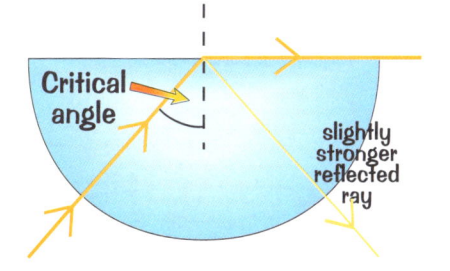

Angle of Incidence EQUAL TO the Critical Angle.
The emerging ray comes out *along the surface*. There's quite a bit of *internal reflection*.

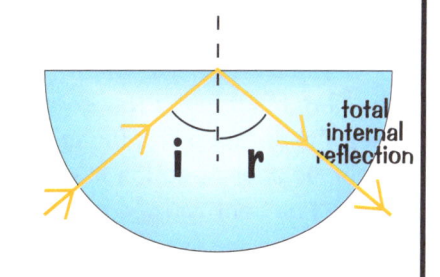

Angle of Incidence GREATER than the Critical Angle.
No light comes out. It's *all* internally reflected, i.e. *total internal reflection*.

1) The *Critical Angle* for *glass* is about 42°. This is *very handy* because it means *45° angles* can be used to get *total internal reflection* as in the *prisms* in the *binoculars* and *periscope* shown on the next page.
2) In *DIAMOND* the *Critical Angle* is much *lower*, about 24°. This is the reason why diamonds *sparkle* so much, because there are lots of *internal reflections*.

Revision — sure it's Critical, but it's not a prism sentence...

First and foremost make sure you can *scribble all the diagrams* down with all the details. Then *scribble a mini-essay* for each topic, jotting down everything you can remember. Then check back and see what you *missed*. Then *learn the stuff you forgot* and *try again*. Ahh... such fun.

Section Three — Waves   AQA Syllabus

Total Internal Reflection

Characteristics of Waves

Binoculars

Total Internal Reflection is used in *binoculars* and *periscopes*. Both use *45° prisms*.

Half a pair of binoculars

Periscope

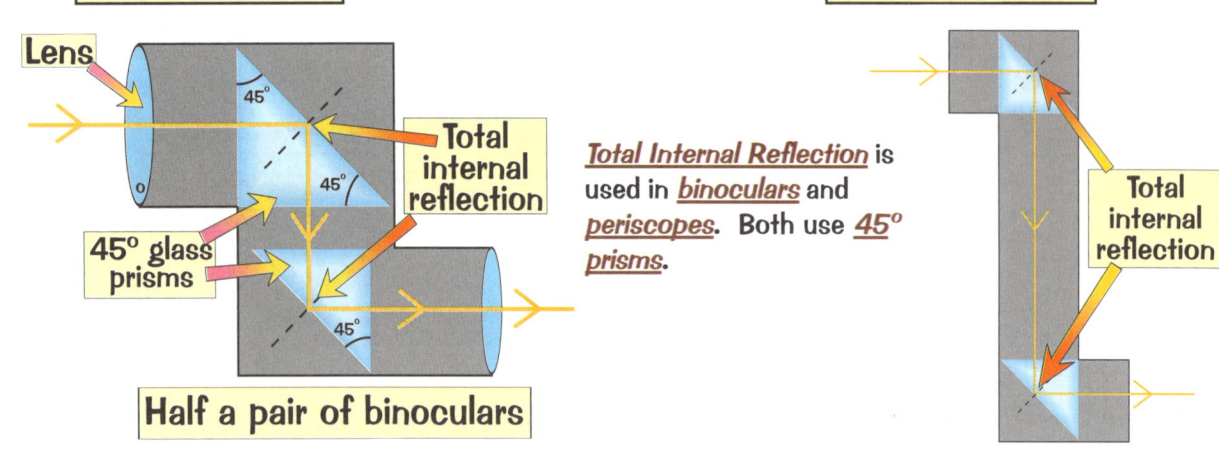

Binoculars and *periscope* use prisms because they give slightly *better reflection* than a *mirror* would and they're also *easier* to hold accurately *in place*. Learn the exact *positioning* of the prisms. They could ask you to *complete* a diagram of a binocular or periscope and unless you've *practised* beforehand you'll find it *pretty tricky* to draw the prisms in *properly*.

Optical Fibres — Communications and Endoscopes

1) *Optical fibres* can carry *information* over *long distances* by repeated *total internal reflections*.
2) Optical communications have several *advantages* over *electrical signals* in wires:
   a) the signal doesn't need *boosting* as often.
   b) a cable of the *same diameter* can carry a lot *more information*.
   c) the signals cannot be *tapped into*, or suffer *interference* from electrical sources.
3) Normally no light whatever would be lost at each reflection. However some light *is lost* due to *imperfections* in the surface, so it still needs *boosting* every *few km*.

The fibre must be *narrow enough* to keep the angles *below* the critical angle, as shown, so the fibre mustn't be bent *too sharply* anywhere.

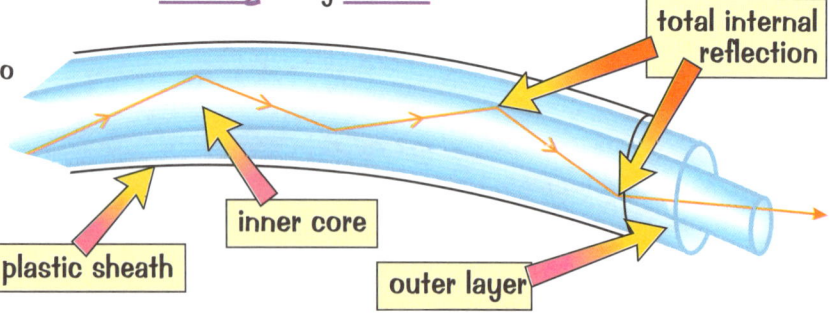

Endoscopes are Used to Look Inside People

This is a *narrow bunch* of *optical fibres* with a *lens system* at each end. Another bunch of optical fibres carries light down *inside* to see with.
The image is displayed as a *full colour moving image* on a TV screen. Real impressive stuff. This means they can do operations *without* cutting big holes in people. This was never possible before optical fibres.

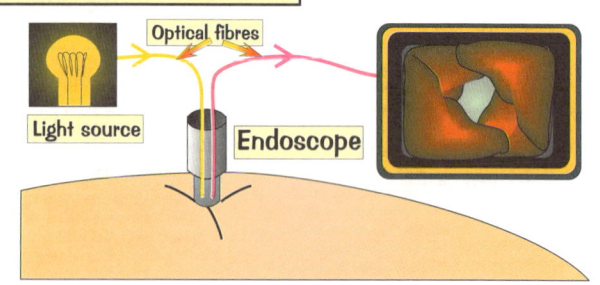

Total Internal Reflection — sounds like a Government Inquiry...

Three sections to learn here, with diagrams for each. They always have *at least one* of these applications of total internal reflection in the Exam. *Learn them all*. None of this is difficult — but just make sure you've got all those little picky details firmly fastened inside your head.

AQA Syllabus

Section Three — Waves

Diffraction

Characteristics of Waves

This word sounds a lot more technical than it really is.

Diffraction is Just the "Spreading Out" of Waves

All waves tend to spread out at the edges when they pass through a gap or past an object. Instead of saying that the wave "spreads out" or "bends" round a corner you should say that it DIFFRACTS around the corner. It's as easy as that. That's all diffraction means.

A Wave Spreads More if it Passes Through a Narrow Gap

The ripple tank shows this effect quite nicely. The same effect applies to light and sound too.

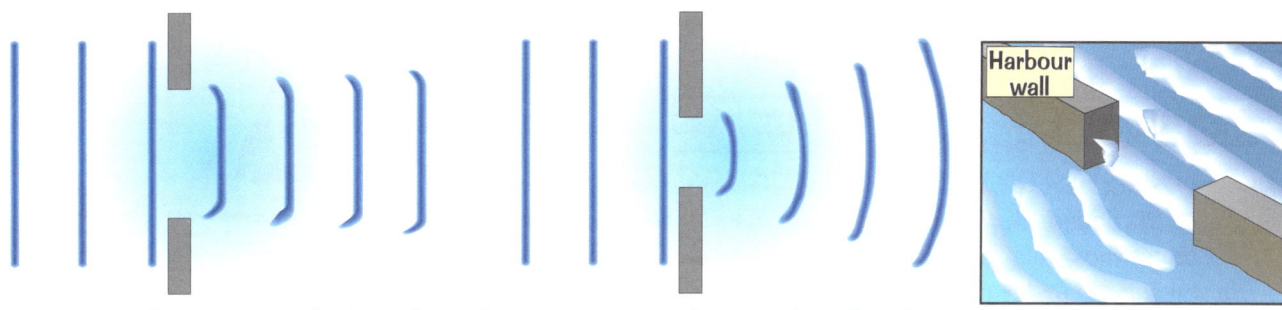

1) A "narrow" gap is one which is about the same size as the wavelength or less.
2) Obviously then, the question of whether a gap is "narrow" or not depends on the wave in question. What may be a narrow gap for a water wave will be a huge gap for a light wave.
3) It should be obvious then, that the longer the wavelength of a wave the more it will diffract.

Sounds Always Diffract Quite a Lot, Because λ is Quite Big

1) Most sounds have wavelengths in air of around 0.1m, which is quite long.
2) This means they spread out round corners so you can still hear people even when you can't see them directly (the sound usually reflects off walls too which also helps).
3) Higher frequency sounds will have shorter wavelengths and so they won't diffract as much, which is why things sound more "muffled" when you hear them from round corners.

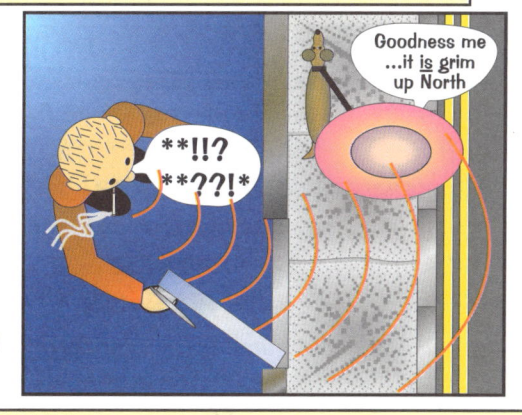

Long Wavelength Radio Waves Diffract Easily Over Hills and into Buildings:

Visible Light on the other hand...

has a very short wavelength, and it'll only diffract with a very narrow slit:

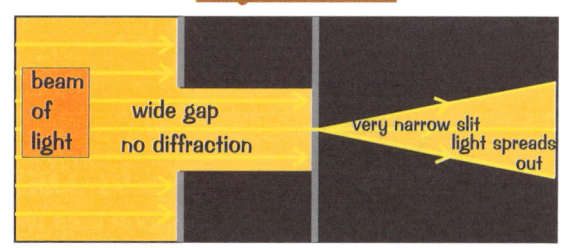

This spreading or diffraction of light (and radio waves) is strong evidence for the wave nature of light.

Diffraction — it can drive you round the bend...

People usually don't know much about diffraction, mainly because there are so few lab demos you can do to show it, and there's also very little to say about it — about one page's worth, in fact. The thing is though, if you just learn this page properly, then you'll know all you need to.

Section Three — Waves *AQA Syllabus*

Using s = d/t and v = fλ

Characteristics of Waves

They're just formulae, *just like all the other formulae*, and the *same old rules apply*.
Mind you, there's a few *extra details* that go with these wave formulae. Learn them now:

The First Rule: Try and Choose the Right Formula

1) People have *way too much difficulty* deciding which *formula* to use.
2) All too often the question starts with "*A wave is travelling...*", and in they leap with "$v = f\lambda$".
3) To choose the *right formula* you have to look for the *THREE quantities* mentioned in the question.
4) If the question mentions *speed*, *frequency* and *wavelength* then sure, "$v = f\lambda$" is the one to use.
5) But if it has *speed*, *time* and *distance* then "$s = d/t$" is more the order of the day — *wouldn't you say*.

Example 1 — Water Ripples

a) Some ripples travel *55cm* in *5 seconds*. Find their speed in cm/s.
   ANSWER: Speed, distance and time are mentioned in the question,
   so we must use "$s=d/t$": $s = d/t = 55/5 = $ *11 cm/s*
b) The wavelength of these waves is found to be *2.2cm*. What is their frequency?
   ANSWER: This time we have f and λ mentioned, so we use "$v = f\lambda$", and we'll need this:
   which tells us that $f = v/\lambda = $ 11cm/s ÷ 2.2cm = *5Hz* (It's very cool to use cm/s with cm, s and Hz)

The Second Rule: Watch those Units — The Little Rascals

1) The *standard (SI) units* involved with waves are: *metres*, *seconds*, *m/s* and *hertz* (Hz).

> Always **CONVERT INTO SI UNITS** (m, s, Hz, m/s) before you work anything out

2) The trouble is waves often have *high frequencies* given in *kHz* or *MHz*, so make sure you *learn this* too:

> 1 kHz (kilohertz) = 1,000 Hz   1 MHz (1 megahertz) = 1,000,000 Hz

3) *Wavelengths* can also be given in *funny* units, e.g. *km* for long wave radio, or *cm* for sound.
4) There's worse still: The *speed of light* is 3×10^8 m/s = *300,000,000 m/s*. This, along with numbers like *900MHz* = *900,000,000 Hz* won't fit into a lot of calculators. That leaves you *three* choices:

   1) Enter the numbers as *standard form* (3×10^8 and 9×10^8), or...
   2) *Cancel* three or six *noughts* off both numbers, (so long as you're *dividing* them!) or...
   3) Do it entirely *without* a calculator! (no really, I've seen it done).   Your choice.

Example 2 — Sound

Q) A sound wave travelling in a solid has a frequency of *19 kHz* and a wavelength of *12cm*. Find its speed.
ANSWER: We have f and λ mentioned, so we'll use "$v = f\lambda$". But we must convert the units into SI:
So, $v = f \times \lambda$ = 19,000Hz × 0.12m = *2,280 m/s*   — convert the units and there's *no problem*.

Example 3 — EM radiation:

Q) A radio wave has a frequency of *92.2 MHz*. Find its wavelength. (The speed of light is 3×10^8 m/s.)
ANSWER: We have f and λ mentioned, so we'll use "$v = f\lambda$". Radio waves travel at the speed of light of course. Once again, we must convert the units into SI, but we'll also have to use standard form:
$\lambda = v/f$ = 3×10^8 / 92,200,000 = 3×10^8 / 9.22×10^7 = *3.25m* (There's a few bits to get wrong)

This stuff on formulae is really painful — I mean it MHz...

Sift out the main rules on this page, then *cover it up* and *scribble them down*. Then try these:
1) A sound wave has a frequency of 2500Hz and a wavelength of 13.2cm. Find its speed.
2) The radio waves for Radio 4 have a wavelength of 1.5 km. Find their frequency.

The E.M. Spectrum
The Electromagnetic Spectrum

There are Seven Basic Types of Electromagnetic Wave

We split Electromagnetic waves (EM waves) into seven basic types as shown below.
These EM waves form a continuous spectrum so the different regions do actually merge into each other.

RADIO WAVES	MICRO WAVES	INFRA RED	VISIBLE LIGHT	ULTRA VIOLET	X-RAYS	GAMMA RAYS
$1m-10^4 m$	$10^{-2} m$ (3cm)	$10^{-5} m$ (0.01mm)	$10^{-7} m$	$10^{-8} m$	$10^{-10} m$	$10^{-12} m$

Our eyes can only detect a very narrow range of EM waves which are the ones we call (visible) light. All EM waves travel at exactly the same speed as light in a vacuum, and pretty much the same speed as light in other media like glass or water — though this is always slower than their speed in vacuum.

When white light is shone through a prism then the colours disperse, due to these fractional changes in speed through the glass medium. You need to learn this diagram and know that violet light bends more than red (See P.29).

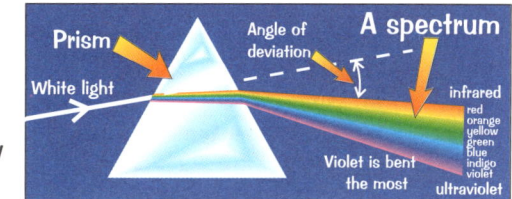

As the Wavelength Changes, so do the Properties

1) As the wavelength of EM radiation changes, its interaction with matter changes. In particular the way any EM wave is absorbed, reflected or transmitted by any given substance depends entirely on its wavelength — that's the whole point of these three pages of course!
2) As a rule the EM waves at each end of the spectrum tend to be able to pass through material, whilst those nearer the middle are absorbed.
3) Also, the ones at the top end (high frequency, short wavelength) tend to be the most dangerous, whilst those lower down are generally harmless.
4) When any EM radiation is absorbed it can cause two effects:
      a) Heating   b) Creation of a tiny alternating current with the same frequency as the radiation.
5) You need to know all the details that follow about all the different part of the EM spectrum:

Radio Waves are Used Mainly for Communications

1) Radio Waves are used mainly for communication and, perhaps more importantly, for controlling model aeroplanes.
2) Both TV and FM Radio use short wavelength radio waves of about 1m wavelength.
3) To receive these wavelengths you need to be more or less in direct sight of the transmitter, because they will not bend (diffract) over hills or travel very far through buildings.
4) The longer wavelengths can travel further because they are reflected from an electrically charged layer in the Earth's upper atmosphere (the ionosphere). This means they can be sent further around the Earth.

The spectrum — isn't that something kinda rude in Biology...

There are lots of details on this page that you definitely need to know. The top diagram is an absolute must — they usually give it you with one or two missing labels to be filled in. Learn the three sections on this page then scribble a mini-essay for each one to see what you know.

Microwaves and Infrared

The Electromagnetic Spectrum

Microwaves Are Used For Cooking and Satellite Signals

1) _Microwaves_ have _two_ main uses: _cooking_ food and _satellite_ transmissions.
2) These two applications use two _different frequencies_ of microwaves.
3) Satellite transmissions use a frequency which _passes easily_ through the _Earth's atmosphere_, including _clouds_, which seems pretty sensible.  
4) The frequency used for _cooking_, on the other hand is one which is readily _absorbed_ by _water molecules_. This is how a microwave oven works. The microwaves pass easily _into the food_ and are then _absorbed_ by the _water molecules_ and turn into heat _inside_ the food.
5) Microwaves can therefore be _dangerous_ because they can be absorbed by _living tissue_ and the heat will _damage or kill_ the cells causing a sort of _"cold burn"_.

Infrared Radiation — Night-Vision and Remote Controls

1) _Infrared_ (or IR) is otherwise known as _heat radiation_. This is given out by all _hot objects_ and you _feel it_ on your _skin_ as _radiant heat_. Infrared is readily _absorbed_ by _all_ materials and _causes heating_.
2) _Radiant heaters_ (i.e. those that _glow red_) use infrared radiation, including _toasters_ and _grills_.
3) _Over-exposure_ to infrared causes _damage_ to cells.
4) Infrared is also used for all the _remote controls_ of _TV's and videos_. It's ideal for sending _harmless_ signals over _short distances_ without _interfering_ with other radio frequencies (like the TV channels).
5) Infrared is also used for _night-vision equipment_. The _police_ use this to spot miscreants _running away_, like you've seen on TV.

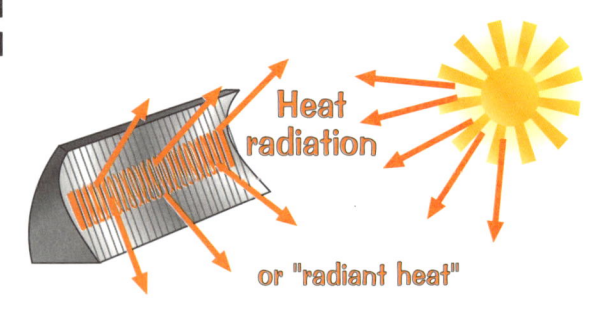

No escape from infrared — if the heat doesn't catch you, the police will...
Each part of the EM spectrum is different, and you definitely need to know all the details about each type of radiation. These are just the kind of things they'll test in your Exams. Do _mini-essays_ for microwaves and IR. Then _check_ to see how you did. Then _try again... and again..._

AQA Syllabus
Section Three — Waves

Visible, UV, X-rays, γ-Rays

The Electromagnetic Spectrum

Visible light is Used To See With and In Optical Fibres

Visible Light is pretty useful. We use it for seeing with for one thing. You could say (as indeed the syllabus does!) that a use of it is in an _endoscope_ for seeing inside a patient's body, but let's face it where do you draw the line? — it's also used in _microscopes_, _telescopes_, _kaleidoscopes_, pretend telescopes made of old toilet rolls, it's used for seeing in the dark (torch, lights etc.) and for saying hi to people without speaking. Seriously though, it is also used in _Optical Fibre Digital Communications_ which is the best one by far for your answer _in the Exam_ (see P.30).

Ultraviolet Light Causes Skin Cancer

1) This is what causes _skin cancer_ if you spend _too much time_ in the _sun_.
2) It also causes your skin to _tan_. _Sunbeds_ give out UV rays but _less harmful ones_ than the Sun does.
3) _Darker skin_ protects against UV rays by _preventing_ them from reaching more vulnerable _skin tissues_ deeper down.
4) There are special _coatings_ which _absorb_ UV light and then _give out visible light_ instead. These are used to coat the inside of _fluorescent tubes_ and lamps.
5) Ultra violet is also useful for hidden _security marks_ which are written in special ink that can only be seen with an ultraviolet light.

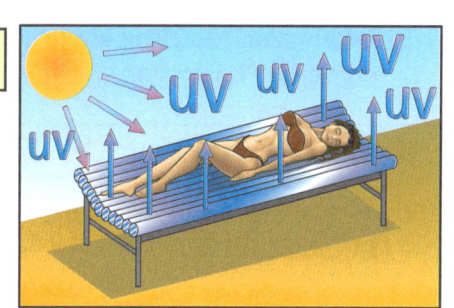

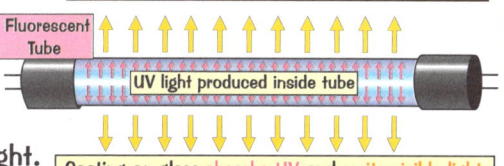

X-Rays are Used in Hospitals, but are Pretty Dangerous

1) These are used in _hospitals_ to take _X-ray photographs_ of people to see whether they have any _broken bones_.
2) X-rays pass easily through _flesh_ but not through _denser material_ such as _bones_ or _metal_.
3) X-rays can cause _cancer_, so _radiographers_, who take X-ray pictures _all day long_ wear _lead aprons_ and stand behind a _lead screen_ to keep their _exposure_ to X-rays to a _minimum_.
4) X-rays can also be used in _scientific research_ to examine the _structure_ of crystals and other materials.

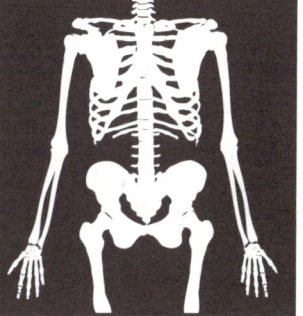

The _brighter bits_ are where _fewer X-rays_ get through. This is a _negative image_. The plate starts off _all white_.

Gamma Rays Cause Cancer but are Used to Treat it Too

1) Gamma rays are used to kill _harmful bacteria_ in food to keep it _fresher for longer_.
2) They are also used to _sterilise medical instruments_, again by _killing the bacteria_.
3) They can also be used in the _treatment of cancer_ because they _kill cancer cells_.
4) Gamma rays tend to _pass through_ soft tissue but _some_ are _absorbed_ by the cells.
5) In _high doses_, gamma rays (along with X-rays and UV rays) can _kill normal cells_.
6) In _lower doses_ all these three types of EM Waves can cause normal cells to become _cancerous_.

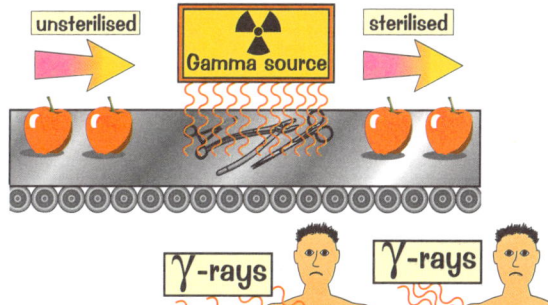

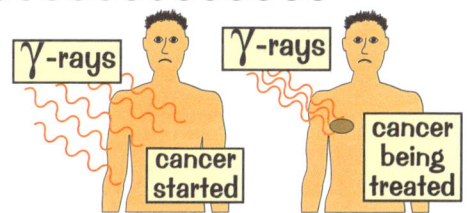

Radiographers are like teachers — they can see right through you...

Here are the other four parts of the EM spectrum for you to learn. Ace, isn't it. At least there's some groovy diagrams to help relieve the tedium. On this page there are four sections. Do a _mini-essay_ for each section, then _check_, _re-learn_, _re-scribble_, _re-check_, etc. etc.

Section Three — Waves
AQA Syllabus

Digital and Analogue Signals

The Electromagnetic Spectrum

You've got to learn the <u>two</u> different ways of transmitting information. Life would be pretty dull without signals — no phones, no computers, even groovy digital watches wouldn't exist.

Information *is Converted Into* Signals

1) Information (e.g. sound, speech, pictures) is converted into <u>electrical signals</u> before it's transmitted.
2) It's then sent long distances down <u>cables</u>, like telephone calls or the internet, or carried on <u>EM waves</u>, like radio or TV.
3) Information can also be sent down <u>optical fibres</u> by converting it into <u>visible light</u> or <u>infrared</u> signals.

Analogue *Varies But* Digital's *Either* On *or* Off

1) The <u>amplitude</u> and <u>frequency</u> of analogue signals <u>vary continuously</u> like in sound waves. Parts of an analogue signal have <u>any</u> value in a range.
2) Dimmer switches, thermometers, speedometers and old fashioned watches are all <u>analogue</u> devices.
3) Digital signals are <u>coded pulses</u> — they have <u>one</u> of only <u>two</u> values: on or off, true or false, 0 or 1...
4) On/off switches, digital clocks and digital meters are <u>digital</u> devices.

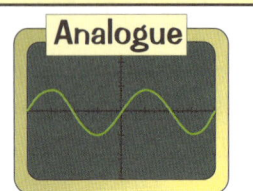

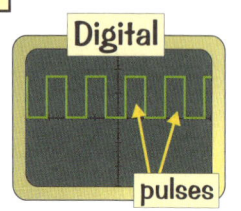

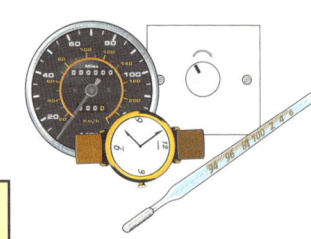

Signals *Have to be* Amplified

Both digital and analogue signals <u>weaken</u> as they travel so they need to be <u>amplified</u> along their route. They also pick up <u>random disturbances</u>, called <u>noise</u>.

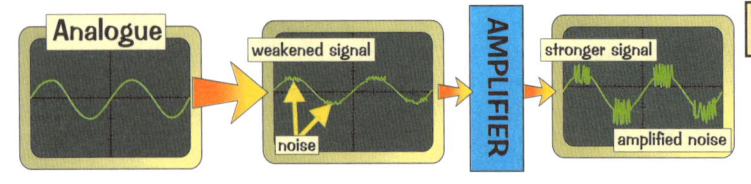

Analogue Signals *Lose* Quality

Each time it's amplified, the analogue signal gets <u>less and less</u> like the original. The different frequencies in it <u>weaken differently</u> at different times — when the signal is amplified, the <u>differences and noise</u> are amplified too.

Digital Signals *Stay the* Same

Noise is usually <u>low amplitude</u> so it's just ignored — it's amplified as OFF. Even a weak signal will still be picked up as an ON pulse so it's amplified as ON. The signal <u>stays exactly the same</u> as the original.

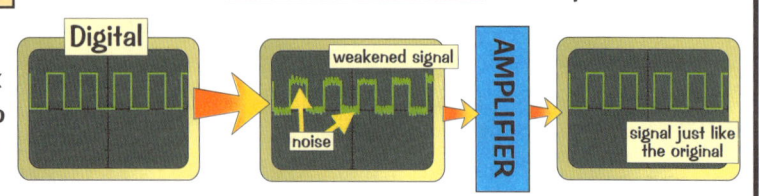

Digital Signals *are* Far Better Quality

1) Digital signals <u>don't change</u> while they're being transmitted. This makes them <u>higher quality</u> — the information transmitted is the <u>same</u> as the original.
2) <u>Loads more information</u> can be sent as digital signals compared to analogue (in a certain time). Many digital signals can be transmitted at once by a clever way of <u>overlapping</u> them on the <u>same</u> cable or EM wave — but you don't need to learn *how* they do it, phew.

<u>Pulses are higher quality — especially those nice Heinz ones...</u>
This stuff follows on neatly from optical fibres so you can bet you'll get a question on it. Make sure you know the <u>differences</u> between digital and analogue signals and <u>why</u> digital ones are better. Learn all the details, then turn the book over and scribble them all down.

AQA Syllabus *Section Three — Waves*

Sound Waves

Sound and Ultrasound

1) Sound travels as a wave:

Sound can be *reflected* off walls (echoes), it can be *refracted* as it passes into different media and it can *diffract* around doors. These are all standard properties of waves so we deduce that *sound travels as a wave*. This "sound" reasoning can also be applied to deduce the wave nature of light.

2) Sound Waves Travel at Various Speeds in Different Media

1) *Sound Waves* are caused by *vibrating* objects.
2) Sound waves are *longitudinal* waves, which travel at *fixed speeds* in particular *media*, as shown in the table.
3) As you can see, the *denser* the medium, the *faster* sound travels through it, generally speaking anyway.
4) Sound generally travels *faster in solids* than in liquids, and faster in liquids than in gases.

Substance	Density	Speed of Sound
Iron	7.9 g/cm^3	5000 m/s
Rubber	0.9 g/cm^3	1600 m/s
Water	1.0 g/cm^3	1400 m/s
Cork	0.3 g/cm^3	500 m/s
Air	0.001 g/cm^3	330 m/s

3) Sound Doesn't Travel Through Vacuum

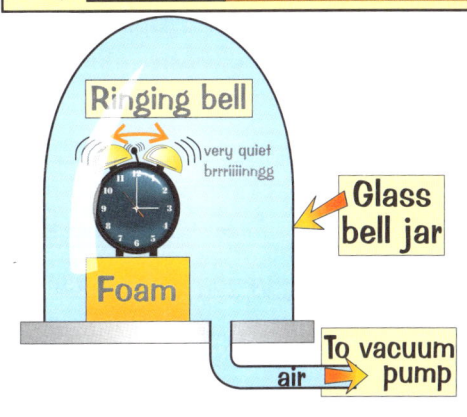

1) Sound waves can be *reflected*, *refracted* and *diffracted*.
2) But one thing they *can't do* is travel through a *vacuum*.
3) This is nicely demonstrated by the jolly old *bell jar experiment*.
4) As the air is *sucked out* by the *vacuum pump*, the sound gets *quieter and quieter*.
5) The bell has to be *mounted* on something like *foam* to stop the sound from it travelling through the solid surface and making the bench vibrate, because you'd hear that instead.

4) Echoes and Reverberation are due to REFLECTED Sound

1) Sound will only be *reflected* from *hard flat surfaces*. Things like *carpets* and *curtains* act as *absorbing surfaces* which will *absorb* sounds rather than reflect them.
2) This is very noticeable in the *reverberation* in an *empty room*. A big empty room sounds *completely different* once you've put carpet and curtains in, and a bit of furniture, because these things absorb the sound quickly and stop it *echoing* (reverberating) around the room.

5) Amplitude is a Measure of the Energy Carried by Any Wave

1) The greater the AMPLITUDE, the *more ENERGY* the wave carries.
2) In SOUND this means it'll be LOUDER.
3) *Bigger amplitude* means a *louder sound*.
4) With LIGHT, a bigger amplitude means it'll be BRIGHTER.

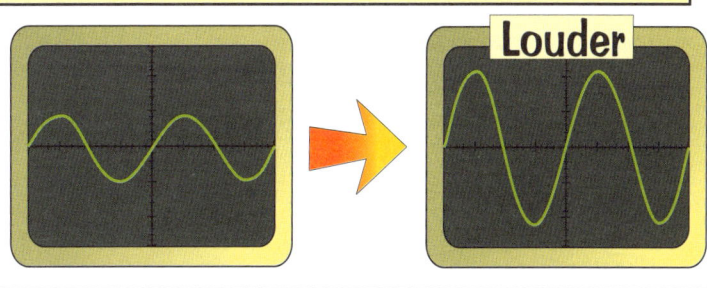

If sound travelled through vacuum — sunny days would be deafening...

Once again the page is broken up into five sections with important numbered points for each. All those numbered points are important. They're all mentioned specifically in the syllabuses so you should expect them to test exactly this stuff in the Exams. *Learn and enjoy*.

Section Three — Waves   *AQA Syllabus*

Frequency and Ultrasound

Sound and Ultrasound

The Frequency of a Sound Wave Determines its Pitch

1) High frequency sound waves sound HIGH PITCHED like a squeaking mouse.
2) Low frequency sound waves sound LOW PITCHED like a mooing cow.
3) Frequency is the number of complete vibrations each second. It's measured in hertz, Hz.
4) Other common units are kHz (1000 Hz) and MHz (1,000,000 Hz).
5) High frequency (or high pitch) also means shorter wavelength.
6) The range of frequencies heard by humans is from 20Hz to 20kHz.
7) These CRO screens are very important so make sure you know all about them:

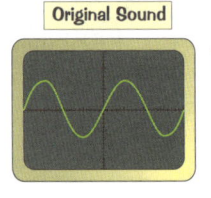

The CRO screens tell us about the pitch and loudness of the sound:

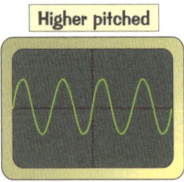

1) The closer the peaks are together, the higher pitched the sound (and the higher the frequency).

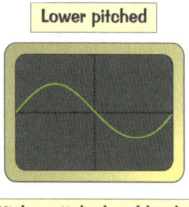

2) When the peaks are further apart then the sound is at a lower pitch (a lower frequency).

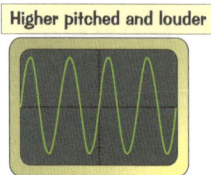

3) The CRO screen will show large peaks for a loud noise (sound waves with a big amplitude).

Ultrasound is Sound with a Higher Frequency than We Can Hear

Electrical devices can be made which produce electrical oscillations of any frequency. These can easily be converted into mechanical vibrations to produce sound waves beyond the range of human hearing (i.e. frequencies above 20kHz). This is called ULTRASOUND and it has loads of uses:

1) Industrial Cleaning of Delicate mechanisms

1) ULTRASOUND CAN BE USED TO CLEAN CASTINGS without them having to be dismantled.
2) The alternatives would either damage the equipment or else it would need to be dismantled first.
3) The same technique is also be used by dentists to remove layers of tartar from teeth.

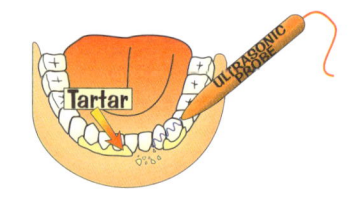

2) Industrial Quality Control

In industrial quality control Ultrasound can be used to detect faulty goods. Any flaws or cracks in the metal castings can be detected with the aid of the ultrasound.

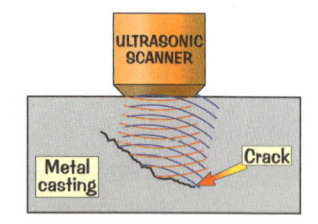

3) For Pre-Natal Scanning of a Foetus

This follows the same principle as the industrial quality control. The Ultrasound waves are used as a safe alternative to X-rays in order to discover if the foetus is healthy or not. The results are processed by computer to produce a video image of the foetus.

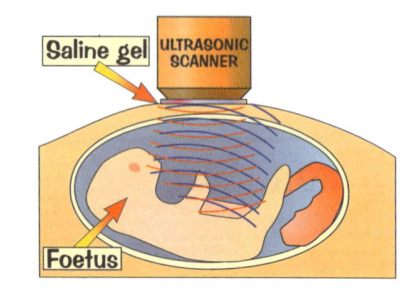

AQA Syllabus

Section Three — Waves

Ultrasonic Detection

Sound and Ultrasound

Detecting with Ultrasound

1) The Ultrasound waves are _transmitted_ through a _metal casting_ and whenever they reach the boundary between two _different media_ (like metal and air) some of the wave is _reflected back_ and detected at the surface. The wave will reflect from the cracks in the casting because of the change in medium from metal to air.
2) The rest of the wave _continues_ through the casting and _more of the wave_ is reflected back (as echoes) at each _boundary_.
3) The exact _timing and distribution_ of these _echoes_ gives detailed _information_ about the internal _structure_ of the casting.
4) The details are then _processed_ by _computer_ to produce a _visual display_ of the casting.

In pre-natal scanning the skin will normally reflect most of the ultrasound so _saline gel_ is used to improve the _transmission_ of the ultrasound through the skin. The sound waves will pass through the skin and _reflect_ from the _surface of the foetus_.
These reflected waves will be _detected_ at the _probe_ and converted into a _visual display_.

Two other uses for ultrasound:

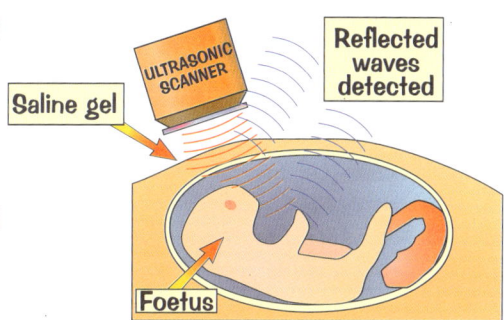

1) Cleaning Delicate Mechanisms

Ultrasound waves in liquids are also used for _cleaning_ delicate mechanisms. The ultrasound waves can be directed on _very precise areas_ and are extremely effective at _removing dirt_ and other deposits which form on _delicate equipment_. The _vibrations_ caused by the ultrasound waves in the liquid _dislodge_ the dirt. The mechanisms do not need to be dismantled in order to clean them in this way.

2) Range and Direction Finding — SONAR

Bats send out _high-pitched squeaks_ (ultrasound) and pick up the _reflections_ with their _big ears_. Their brains are able to _process_ the reflected signal and turn it into a _picture_ of what's around.
So the bats basically "_see_" with _sound waves_, well enough in fact to catch _moths_ in _mid-flight_ in complete _darkness_ — it's a nice trick if you can do it.

The same technique is used for _SONAR_ which uses _sound waves underwater_ to detect features on the sea-bed. The _pattern_ of the reflections indicates the _depth_ and basic features.

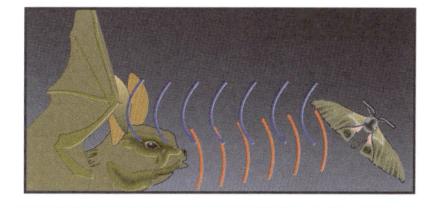

Ultrasound — weren't they a pop group...

Geesh — *a double* page on sound and with seven sections in total. No numbered points this time though. That means the mini-essay method is going to be a better idea. _Learn_ the seven headings, then _cover the pages_ and _scribble a mini-essay_ for each, with diagrams. Enjoy.

Section Three — Waves

AQA Syllabus

The Speed of Sound

Sound and Ultrasound

Relative Speeds of Sound and Light

1) *Light* travels about *a million times faster* than *sound*, so you never bother to calculate how long it takes compared to sound. You only work out the time taken for the *sound* to travel.
2) The *formula* needed is always the good old *s*d*t* one for *speed, distance and time* (see P. 17).
3) When something makes a sound more than about *100m away* and you can actually *see* the action which makes the sound then the effect is quite *noticeable*. Good examples are:
   a) *LIVE CRICKET* — you hear the "*knock*" a while after seeing the ball being struck.
   b) *HAMMERING* — you hear the "*clang*" when the hammer is back up *in mid air*.
   c) *STARTING PISTOL* — you *see the smoke* and then *hear the bang*.
   d) *JET AIRCRAFT* — they're always *ahead* of where it sounds like they are.
   e) *THUNDER AND LIGHTNING* — the flash of lightning causes the sound of the thunder, and the *time interval* between the *flash* and the *rumble* tells you how far away the lightning is. There's approximately *five seconds delay for every mile*. (1 mile = 1600m, ÷ 330 = 4.8s)

EXAMPLE: *Looking out from his modest office across the Designated (EU Directive 672) Young Persons Recreation Area (i.e. the school yard), the Headmaster saw the five most troublesome and nauseating kids in his school destroying something nice with their horrid hammer. Before acting swiftly, he did take the time to notice that there was a delay of exactly 0.4 seconds between the hammer striking and the sound reaching his shell-like ear. So just how far away were these horrid children? (Sound travels at 330m/s in air, as you know.)*

ANSWER: The formula we want is of course "Speed = Distance/Time" or "s=d/t".
We want to find the distance, d. We already know the time is 0.4s,
and the speed of sound in air = 330m/s. Hence d=s×t (from the triangle)
This gives: d = 330×0.4 = *132m*. (That's how far the sound travels in 0.4 secs.) Easy peasy.

Echo Questions — Don't Forget the Factor of Two

1) The *big thing* to remember with *echo questions* is that because the sound has to travel *both ways*, then to get the *right answer* you'll need to either *double something* or *halve something*.
2) Make sure you remember: sound travels at about *330m/s in air* and *1400m/s in water*.
Any echo question will likely be in air or water and if you have to work out the speed of the sound it's real useful to know what sort of number you should be getting.
So for example, if you get 170m/s for the speed of sound in air then you should realise you've *forgotten the factor of two* somewhere, and then you can *easily go back and sort it*.

EXAMPLE: *Having successfully expelled the five most troublesome and nauseating kids from his school, the jubilant Headmaster popped open a bottle of Champagne and heard the echo 0.6s later from the other side of his modest office. Just how big was this modest office?*

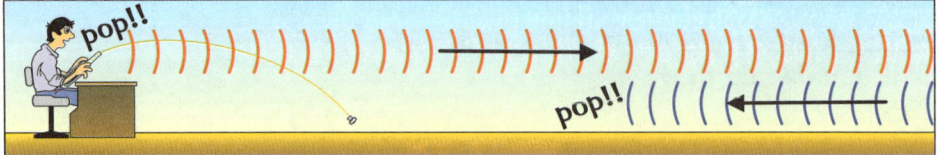

ANSWER: The formula is of course "Speed = Distance/Time" or "s=d/t". We want to find the distance, d.
We already know the time, 0.6s, and the speed (of sound in air), hence d=s×t (from triangle)
This gives: d = 330×0.6 = *198m*. But Watch out! *Don't forget the factor of two for echo questions:*
The 0.6 secs is for *there and back*, so the office is only *half* that distance, *99m long*.

Learn about Echoes and the Factor of Two...Factor of Two...Factor of Two...

Learn the details on this page, then *cover it up* and *scribble them down*. Then try these:
1) A man sees the cricketer hit the ball and hears the knock 0.6s later. How far away is he?
2) A ship sends a sonar signal to the sea bed and detects the echo 0.7s later. How deep is it?

AQA Syllabus

Section Three — Waves

Seismic Waves

Seismic Waves Are Caused By Earthquakes

1) We can only drill about 10km or so into the crust of the Earth, which is not very far, so seismic waves are really the only way of investigating the inner structure.
2) When there's an Earthquake somewhere the shock waves travel out from it and we detect them all over the surface of the planet using seismographs.
3) We measure the time it takes for the two different types of shock wave to reach each seismograph.
4) We also note the parts of the Earth which don't receive the shock waves at all.
5) From this information you can work out all sorts of stuff about the inside of the Earth as shown below:

S-Waves and P-Waves Take Different Paths

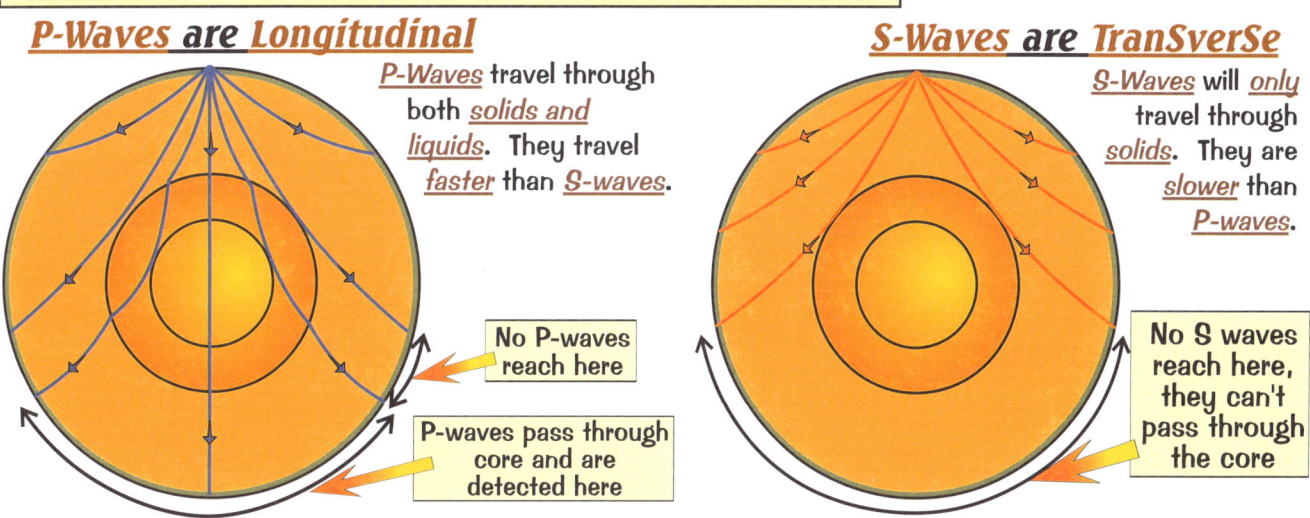

P-Waves are Longitudinal

P-Waves travel through both solids and liquids. They travel faster than S-waves.

No P-waves reach here

P-waves pass through core and are detected here

S-Waves are TranSverSe

S-Waves will only travel through solids. They are slower than P-waves.

No S waves reach here, they can't pass through the core

The Seismograph Results Tell Us What's Down There

1) About halfway through the Earth, there's an abrupt change in direction of both types of wave. This indicates that there's a sudden increase in density at that point — the CORE.
2) The fact that S-waves are not detected in the shadow of this core tells us that it's very liquid.
3) It's also found that P-waves travel slightly faster through the middle of the core, which strongly suggests that there's a solid inner core.
4) Note that S-waves do travel through the mantle which suggests that it's kinda solid, though I always thought it was made of molten lava which looks pretty liquidy to me when it comes sploshing out of volcanoes. Still there you go, just another one of life's little conundrums, I guess.

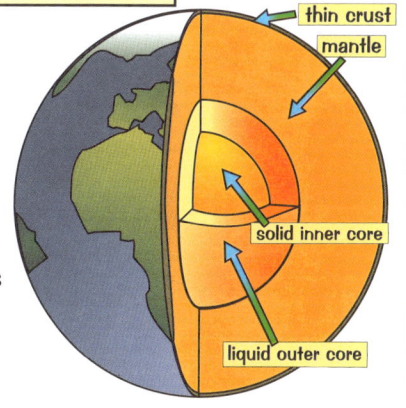

thin crust, mantle, solid inner core, liquid outer core

The Paths Curve Due to Increasing Density (causing Refraction)

1) Both S-waves and P-waves travel faster in more dense material.
2) The curvature of their paths is due to the increasing density of the mantle and core with depth.
3) When the density changes suddenly, the waves change direction abruptly, as shown above.
4) The paths curve because the density of both the mantle and the core increases steadily with increasing depth. The waves gradually change direction because their speed is gradually changing, due to gradual changes in the density of the medium. This is refraction, of course.

Seismic Waves — they reveal the terrible trembling truth...

The last page on waves. Hoorah. Once again there are four main sections to learn. Learn the headings first, then try scribbling down all the details for each heading, including the diagrams. Remember that S-waves are tranSverSe — so P-waves must be the longitudinal ones.

Section Three — Waves *AQA Syllabus*

Evidence for Plate Tectonics

Tectonics

The Earth's Surface is made up of Large Plates of Rock

1) The Earth's lithosphere is the crust and the upper part of the mantle. It's cracked into pieces called plates.
2) These plates are like big rafts that float across the liquid mantle.
3) The map shows the edges of these plates. As they move, the continents move too. The movement of the plates is known as Plate Tectonics.
4) The plates are moving at a speed of about 1cm or 2cm per year.

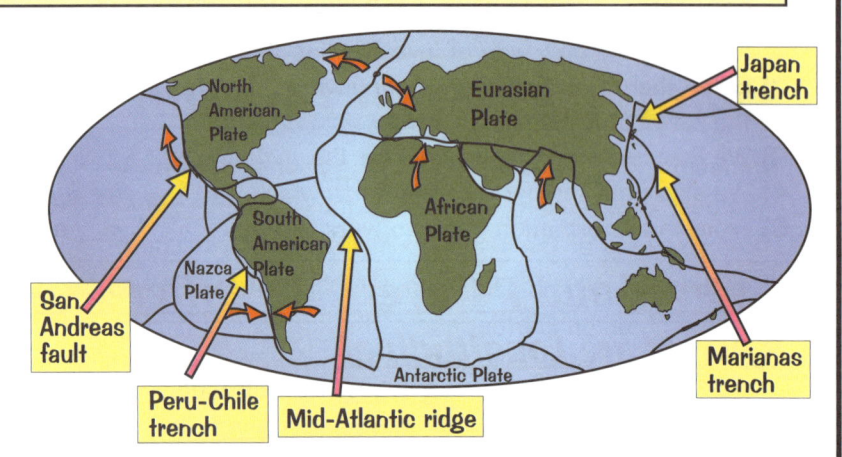

Evidence for Plate Tectonics

1) Jigsaw Fit — the supercontinent "Pangaea"

a) There's a very obvious jigsaw fit between Africa and South America.
b) The other continents can also be fitted in without too much trouble.
c) It's widely believed that they once all formed a single land mass, now called Pangaea.

2) Matching Fossils in Africa and South America

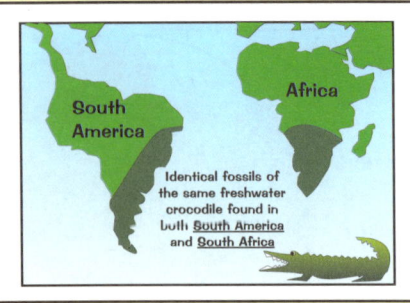

a) Identical plant fossils of the same age have been found in rocks in South Africa, Australia, Antarctica, India and South America, which strongly suggests they were all joined once upon a time.
b) Animal fossils support the theory too. There are identical fossils of a freshwater crocodile found in both Brazil and South Africa. It certainly didn't swim across.

3) Identical Rock Sequences

a) There is remarkable similarity between rock strata of similar ages in various countries.
b) This is strong evidence that these countries were joined together when the rocks formed.

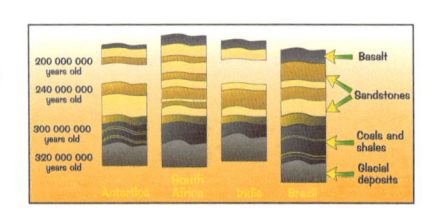

Wegener's Theory of Crustal Movement

In 1915 Alfred Wegener proposed his "continental drift" theory — that the continents had once been joined but were slowly drifting apart. No one believed him until the 1960s when fossil evidence and the magnetic pattern of the mid-Atlantic ridge (see P.44) backed up his theory.

Learn about Plate Tectonics — but don't get carried away...

These three bits of evidence plus the bits on the next two pages all support Wegener's theory. This is a pretty big topic so it all needs to go into your grey cells. Make sure you can explain Wegener's Theory, including why it wasn't accepted at first. Learn, cover, scribble, etc...

AQA Syllabus Section Three — Waves

Plate Boundaries

Tectonics

At the boundaries between tectonic plates there's usually trouble like volcanoes or earthquakes. There are three different ways that plates interact: Colliding, separating or sliding past each other.

Plates Sliding Past Each Other: San Francisco

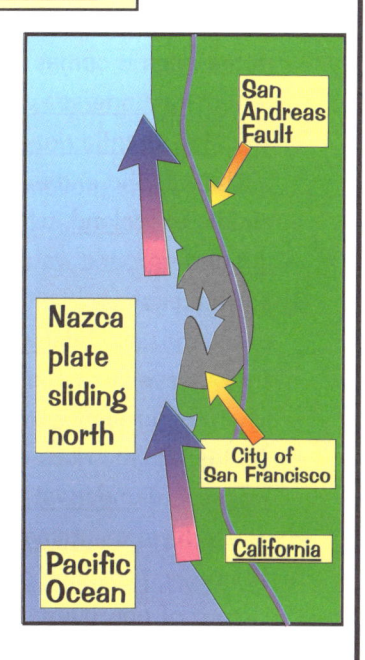

1) Sometimes the plates are just sliding past each other.
2) The best known example of this is the San Andreas Fault in California.
3) A narrow strip of the coastline is sliding north at about 7cm a year.
4) Big plates of rock don't glide smoothly past each other.
5) They catch on each other and as the forces build up they suddenly lurch.
6) This sudden lurching only lasts a few seconds — but it'll bring buildings down, no problem.
7) The city of San Francisco sits astride this fault line. (They didn't know that when they built it!)
8) The city was destroyed by an earthquake in 1906 and hit by another quite serious one in 1989. They could have another one any time.
9) In earthquake zones they try to build earthquake-proof buildings which are designed to withstand a bit of shaking.
10) Earthquakes usually cause much greater devastation in poorer countries where they may have overcrowded cities, poorly constructed buildings, and inadequate rescue services.

Oceanic and Continental Plates Colliding: The Andes

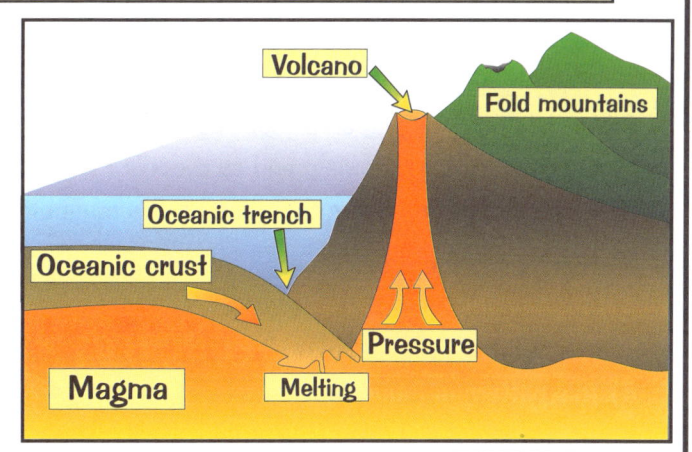

1) The oceanic plate is always forced underneath the continental plate.
2) This is called a subduction zone.
3) As the oceanic crust is pushed down it melts and pressure builds up due to all the melting rock.
4) This molten rock finds its way to the surface and volcanoes form.
5) There are also earthquakes as the two plates slowly grind past each other.
6) A deep trench forms on the ocean floor where the oceanic plate is being forced down.
7) The continental crust crumples and folds forming mountains at the coast.
8) The classic example of all this is the west coast of South America where the Andes mountains are. That region has all the features:

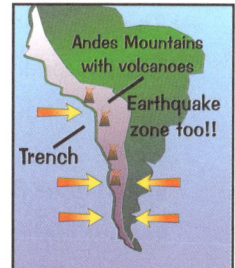

Volcanoes, earthquakes, an oceanic trench and mountains.

Another page to learn — don't make a mountain out of it...

Make sure you learn all these diagrams — they summarise all the information in the text. They may well ask you for examples in the Exam, so make sure you know the two different kinds of situation that the Andes and San Francisco actually represent. Cover and scribble...

Section Three — Waves *AQA Syllabus*

Plate Boundaries

Tectonics

Sea Floor Spreading 1: The mid-Atlantic Ridge

1) When tectonic plates move apart, magma rises up to fill the gap and produces new crust made of basalt (of course). Sometimes it comes out with great force producing undersea volcanoes.
2) The Mid-Atlantic ridge runs the whole length of the Atlantic and actually cuts through the middle of Iceland, which is why they have hot underground water.
3) Earthquakes and volcanoes under the sea can cause massive tidal waves (tsunamis). These waves can cause great destruction when they reach land.
4) As the magma rises up through the gap it forms ridges and underwater mountains.
5) These form a symmetrical pattern either side of the ridge, providing strong evidence for the theory of continental drift.

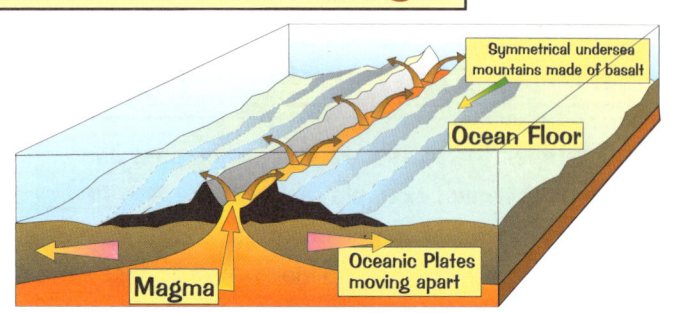

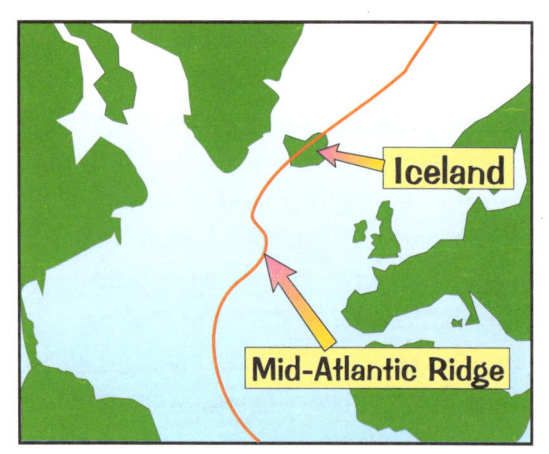

Sea Floor Spreading 2: Magnetic Reversal Patterns

1) However the most compelling evidence in favour of continental drift comes from the magnetic orientation of the rocks.
2) As the liquid magma erupts out of the gap, the iron particles in the rocks tend to align themselves with the Earth's magnetic field and as it cools they set in position.
3) Every half million years or so the Earth's magnetic field tends to swap direction.
4) This means the rock on either side of the ridge has bands of alternate magnetic polarity.
5) This pattern is found to be symmetrical either side of the ridge.
6) These magnetic stripes were only discovered in the 1960s.
7) These stripes spread out at a rate of about 2 cm per year, which is pretty slow. In fact, continents move at pretty much the same speed your fingernails grow at. It's sad, but you probably won't observe any continental drift in your lifetime!

Sea Floor Spreading — Learn the Shocking Truth...

The stuff on this page + the stuff on page 42 provides all the evidence supporting Wegener's Theory. Learn all of it well enough to be able to answer a question like this: "Describe evidence which supports the theory of Plate Tectonics" (5 marks). Mini-essay time.

AQA Syllabus   *Section Three — Waves*

Revision Summary for Section Three

Most of this stuff is fairly easy and just needs learning. This book contains all the important information that's specifically mentioned in the syllabus — the stuff they're going to test you on in the Exams. You must practise these questions over and over again until they're easy.

1) Sketch a wave and mark on it the amplitude and wavelength.
2) Define frequency, amplitude and wavelength for a wave.
3) Sketch a transverse wave. Give a definition for it. Give four examples of transverse waves.
4) Sketch a longitudinal wave. Give a definition for it. Give two examples of longitudinal waves.
5) Give three examples of waves carrying energy.
6) Sketch the patterns when plane ripples reflect at a) a plane surface, b) a curved surface.
7) Sketch the reflection of curved ripples at a plane surface.
8) What is the law of reflection? Are sound and light reflected?
9) Draw a neat ray diagram to show how to locate the position of the image in a plane mirror.
10) What is refraction? What causes it? How does it affect wavelength and frequency?
11) Sketch a ray of light going through a rectangular glass block, showing the angles i and r.
12) How fast does light go in glass? Which way does it bend as it enters glass? What if i=90°?
13) What is dispersion? Sketch the diagram which illustrates it with all the labels.
14) Sketch the three diagrams to illustrate Total Internal Reflection and the Critical Angle.
15) Sketch two applications of total internal reflection which use 45° prisms, and explain them.
16) Give details of the two main uses of optical fibres. How do optical fibres work?
17) What is diffraction? Sketch the diffraction of a) water waves b) sound waves c) light.
18) What are the two formulas involved with waves? How do you decide which one to use?
19) Are SI units important? What are the SI units for: wavelength; frequency; velocity; time?
20) Convert these to SI units: a) 500kHz, b) 35cm, c) 4.6MHz, d) 4cm/s, e) 2½ mins.
21) Find the speed of a wave with frequency 50kHz and wavelength 0.3cm.
22) Find the frequency of a wave of wavelength 1.5km and speed 3×10^8 m/s.
23) What aspect of EM waves determines their differing properties?
24) Sketch the EM spectrum with all its details. What happens when EM waves are absorbed?
25) Give full details of the uses of radio waves.
26) Give full details of the two main uses of microwaves, and the three main uses of infrared.
27) Give a sensible example of the use of visible light. What is its main use?
28) Detail three uses of UV light, two uses of X-rays and three uses of gamma rays.
29) What harm will UV, X-rays and gamma rays do in *high* doses? What about in *low* doses?
30) What's the difference between analogue and digital signals? Which is the best and why?
31) Describe the bell jar experiment. What does it demonstrate?
32) What's an echo? What is reverberation? What affects reverberation in a room?
33) What effect does greater amplitude have on a) sound waves b) light waves?
34) What's the relationship between frequency and pitch for a sound wave?
35) Sketch CRO screens showing higher and lower pitch and quiet and loud sounds.
36) What is ultrasound? Give details of two applications of ultrasound.
37) Describe how Ultrasound is used to find flaws in materials.
38) How do the speeds of sound and light compare? Give five examples where you notice this.
39) A crash of thunder is heard 6 seconds after the flash of lightning. How far away is it?
40) If the sea bed is 600m down, how long will it take to receive a sonar echo from it?
41) What causes seismic waves? Sketch diagrams showing the paths of both types, and explain.
42) What do seismographs tell us about the structure of the Earth? Describe the Earth's inner structure.
43) Give three pieces of evidence for Plate Tectonics.
44) What happens when a) plates slide past each other and b) they collide?
45) How does the magnetic orientation of rocks give evidence for continental drift?

Section Three — Waves   *AQA Syllabus*

The Earth & Beyond

The Cause of Days and Seasons

The Solar System

The Rotation of The Earth Causes Day and Night

1) As the Earth slowly <u>rotates</u> any point on the Earth's surface moves from the <u>bright side</u> in the <u>sunlight</u> round into the <u>darkness</u>. As the Earth keeps rotating it eventually comes back into the sunshine again. This sequence describes <u>day-dusk-night-dawn</u>.

2) A <u>full rotation</u> takes <u>24 hours</u> of course — a full day. Next time you watch the <u>Sun set</u>, try to <u>imagine yourself</u> helpless on that <u>big rotating ball</u> as you move silently across the <u>twilight zone</u> and into the <u>shadows</u>.

3) Also notice that because of the <u>tilt</u> of the axis, places in the <u>Northern Hemisphere</u> are spending <u>much longer</u> in the <u>sunshine</u> than in the <u>shade</u> (night time), whereas places in the <u>Southern Hemisphere</u> are spending more time in the <u>dark</u>. This is only because of the <u>time of year</u>. See below.

4) Also notice that the further towards the <u>Poles</u> you get, the <u>longer</u> the days are in <u>summer</u> and the longer the <u>nights</u> are in <u>winter</u>. Places *inside* the <u>arctic circle</u> have <u>24 hours a day</u> of sunlight for a few days in <u>mid summer</u>, whilst in <u>mid winter</u> the Sun <u>never rises</u> at all.

5) At the <u>Equator</u> by contrast, the length of day <u>never varies</u> from one season to the next. It's always <u>12 hours of day</u> and <u>12 hours of night</u>. The position of the <u>shadows</u> shows all this.

The Orbit of the Earth around the Sun takes 365¼ days

One <u>full orbit</u> of the Earth around the Sun is <u>approximately 365 days</u> (one year). This is split up into <u>the seasons</u>:

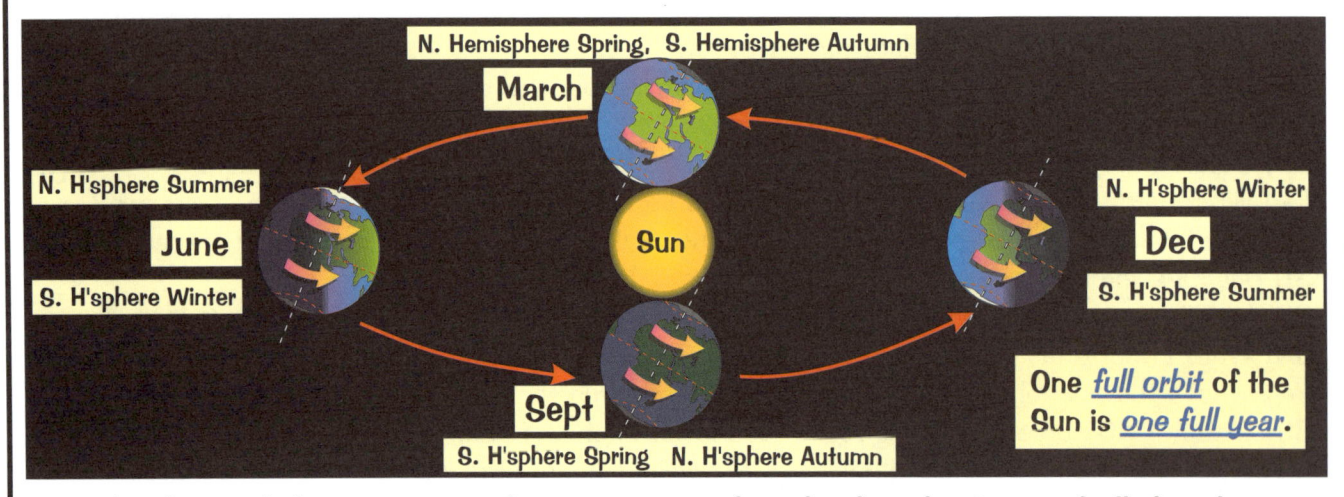

In the dim and distant past <u>early astronomers</u> thought that the Sun and all the planets <u>orbited the Earth</u>, i.e. that the Earth was the <u>centre of the Universe</u>.
As we all know this was <u>very wrong</u>, but then they also thought the Earth was flat, and that the Moon was made of cheese.

See Norway at Christmas — take a good torch...

This stuff about what causes the Sun to seem to "rise" and "set" and how the seasons are caused is surely irresistible-just-gotta-know-all-about-it kind of information, isn't it? Surely you must be filled with burning curiosity about it every time the dawn breaks — aren't you?

AQA Syllabus — *Section Four — The Earth & Beyond*

The Solar System

The _order_ of the planets can be remembered by using the little jollyism below:

Mercury,	Venus,	Earth,	Mars,	(Asteroids),	Jupiter,	Saturn,	Uranus,	Neptune,	Pluto
(My	Very	Energetic	Maiden	Aunt	Just	Swam	Under	North	Pier)

MERCURY, _VENUS_, _EARTH_ and _MARS_ are known as the _INNER PLANETS_.
JUPITER, _SATURN_, _URANUS_, _NEPTUNE_ and _PLUTO_ are much further away and are the _OUTER PLANETS_.

The Planets Don't Give Out Light, They just Reflect The Sun's

1) You can _see_ some of the nearer planets with the _naked eye_ at night, e.g. Mars and Venus.
2) They look just like _stars_, but they are of course _totally different_.
3) Stars are _huge_ and _very far away_ and _give out_ lots of light.
   The planets are _smaller and nearer_ and they just _reflect the sunlight_ falling on them.
4) Planets always _orbit around stars_. In our Solar System the planets orbit the _Sun_ of course.
5) These orbits are all _slightly elliptical_ (elongated circles).
6) All the planets in our Solar System orbit in the _same plane_ except Pluto (as shown).

The Sun is a Star, Giving Out All Types of EM Radiation

1) The Sun, like other stars produces _heat_ from _nuclear fusion reactions_ which turn _hydrogen into helium_. This makes it really hot.
2) It gives out the _full spectrum_ of _electromagnetic radiation_.

The Relative Sizes of the Planets and Sun

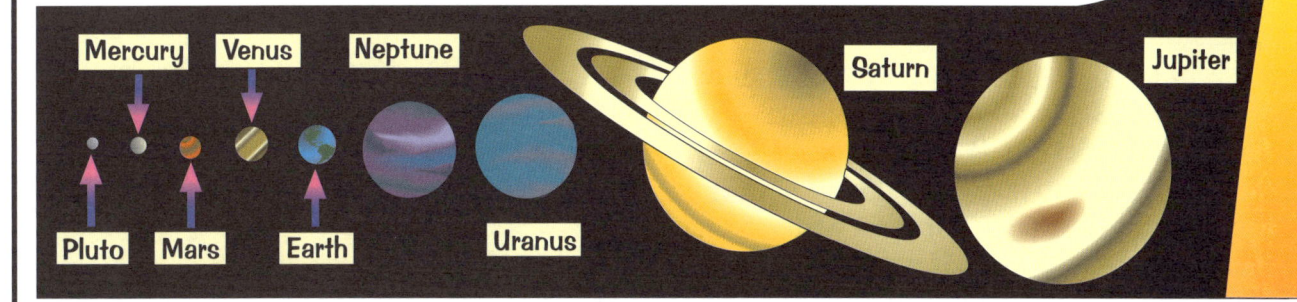

Learn the Planets — they can be quite illuminating...

Isn't the Solar System great! All those pretty coloured planets and all that big black empty space. You can look forward to one or two easy questions on the planets — or you might get two real horrors instead. Be ready, _learn_ all the _nitty-gritty details_ till you know it all real good.

Section Four — The Earth & Beyond

The Planets

The Solar System

Some Data on Planets which you Need to Kind of Know About

That doesn't mean you should learn every number, but you should definitely have a pretty good idea which planets are biggest, or furthest out etc. This table is a summary of the most important data on planets:

	PLANET	DIAMETER (km)	MASS	MEAN DIST. FROM SUN	ORBIT TIME	
INNER PLANETS	MERCURY	4 800	0.05	58	88d	
	VENUS	12 100	0.8 (Earth	108 (millions	225d	d=Earth
	EARTH	12 800	1.0 masses)	150 of km)	365d	days
	MARS	6 800	0.1	228	687d	
OUTER PLANETS	JUPITER	143 000	318.0	778	12y	
	SATURN	120 000	95.0	1430	29y	y=Earth
	URANUS	51 000	15.0	2870	84y	years
	NEPTUNE	49 000	17.0	4500	165y	
	PLUTO	2 400	0.003	5900	248y	

Gravity Is the Force which Keeps Everything in Orbit

1) *Gravity* is a force of *attraction* which acts between *all* masses.
2) With *very large* masses like *stars* and *planets*, the force is *very big* and acts *a long way out*.
3) The *closer* you get to a planet, the *stronger* the *force of attraction*.
4) To *counteract* this stronger gravity, the planet must move *faster* and cover its orbit *quicker*.
5) *Comets* are also held in *orbit* by gravity, as are *moons* and *satellites* and *space stations*.

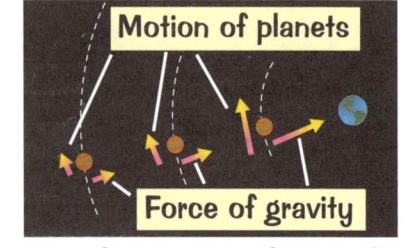

Motion of planets
Force of gravity

Planets in the Night Sky Seem to Move across the Constellations

1) The stars in the sky form *fixed patterns* called *constellations*.
2) These all stay *fixed* in *relation to each other* and simply "*rotate*" as the Earth spins.
3) The *planets* look *just like stars* except that they *wander* across the constellations over periods of *days or weeks*, often going in the *opposite direction*.
4) Their position and movement depends on where they are *in their orbit*, compared to us.
5) This *peculiar movement* of the planets made the early astronomers realise that the Earth *wasn't the centre of the Universe* after all, but was in fact just *the third rock from the Sun*. It's *very strong evidence* for the *Sun-centred* model of the Solar System.
6) Alas, the boys at *The Spanish Inquisition* were less than keen on such heresy, and poor old *Copernicus* had a pretty hard time of it for a while. In the end though, "*the truth will out*".

Learn this page — but keep shtum to the boys in the Red Robes...

Planets are ace aren't they. There's all that exciting data to sort of be vaguely familiar with for a start. Then there's the fact that you can see one or two of them in the night sky, just by lifting your eyes to the heavens. *Learn* all the other details on this page too, then *cover and scribble*.

Satellites

The Solar System

1) Moons are sometimes called Natural Satellites

The planets in our solar system are all *natural satellites* of the Sun. The planets also have their own natural satellites (moons):

1) The Earth only has *one moon* of course, but some of the *other planets* have *quite a few*.
2) We can only *see* the Moon because it *reflects sunlight*.
3) The *phases of the Moon* happen depending on where the moon is in its orbit. The position of the Moon determines *how much* of its *illuminated side* we can *see*:

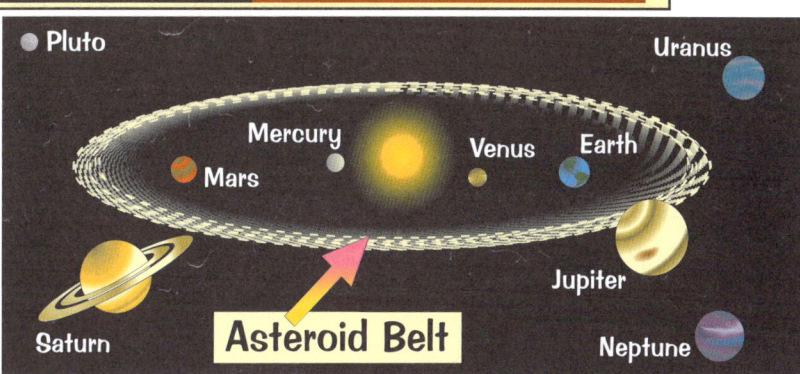

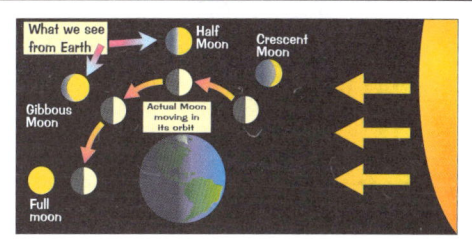

All satellites *in orbit* about a body, be they artificial or natural, have to move at a *certain speed* to stay in orbit at a *certain distance*. The *greater* the distance away the *longer* it takes to complete a *full orbit*. This also means that the *further* away then the *slower* the satellite must travel to *maintain its orbit*.

2) Artificial Satellites are very useful

Artificial satellites are sent up by humans for *four main purposes*:

1) Monitoring *Weather*.
2) *Communications*, e.g. phone and TV.
3) *Space research* such as the Hubble Telescope.
4) *Spying* on baddies.

There are *two different orbits* useful for satellites:

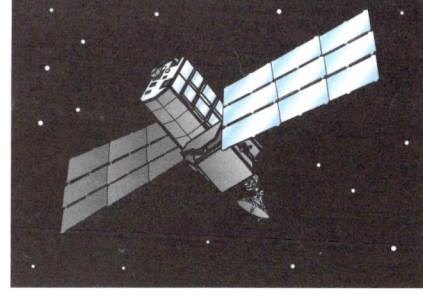

3) Geostationary Satellites are Used for Communications

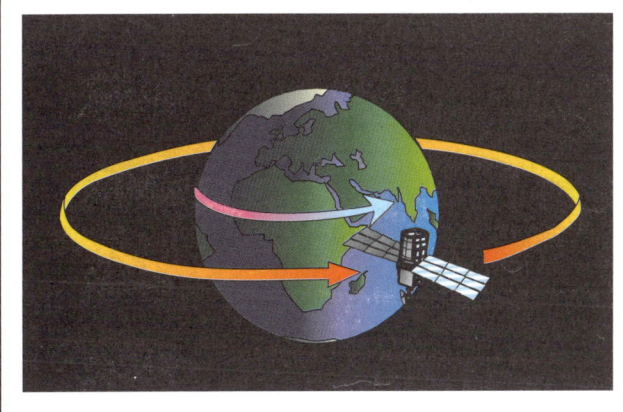

1) These can also be called *geosynchronous satellites*.
2) They are put in quite a *high orbit* over the *Equator* which takes *exactly 24 hours* to complete.
3) This means that they stay *above the same point* on the Earth's surface because the Earth *rotates with them* — hence the name Geo-(Earth)stationary.
4) This makes them *ideal* for *Telephone and TV* because they're always in the *same place* and they can *transfer signals* from one side of the Earth to another in a *fraction of a second*.

Section Four — The Earth & Beyond   *AQA Syllabus*

Satellites and Comets

The Solar System

4) Low Polar Orbit Satellites are for Weather and Spying

1) In a low polar orbit the satellite sweeps over both poles whilst the Earth rotates beneath it.
2) The time taken for each full orbit is just a few hours.
3) Each time the satellite comes round it can scan the next bit of the globe.
4) This allows the whole surface of the planet to be monitored each day.
5) Geostationary satellites are too high to take good weather or spying photos, but the satellites in polar orbits are nice and low.

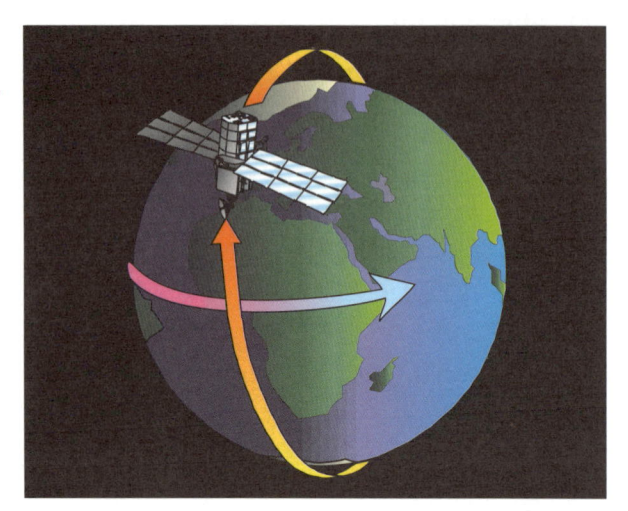

5) The Hubble Telescope has no Atmosphere in the way

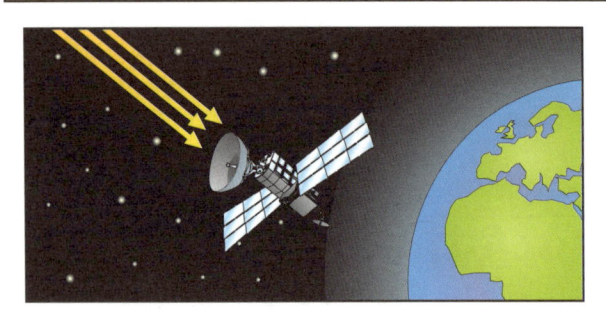

1) The big advantage of having telescopes on satellites is that they can look out into space without the distortion and blurring caused by the Earth's atmosphere.
2) This allows much greater detail to be seen of distant stars and also the planets in the Solar System.

Comets Orbit the Sun, but have very Eccentric (elongated) Orbits

1) Comets only appear every few years because their orbits take them very far from the Sun and then back in close, which is when we see them.
2) The Sun is not at the centre of the orbit but near to one end as shown.
3) Comet orbits can be in different planes from the orbits of the planets.
4) Comets are made of ice and rock and as they approach the Sun the ice melts leaving a bright tail of debris which can be millions of km long.
5) The comet travels much faster when it's nearer the Sun than it does when it's in the more distant part of its orbit.
This is because the pull of gravity makes it speed up as it gets closer, and then slows it down as it gets further away from the Sun.

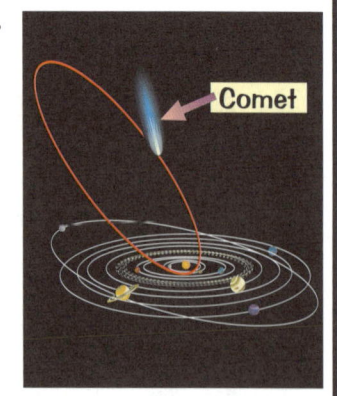

Learn about Satellites — and look down on your friends...

You can actually see the low polar orbit satellites on a nice dark clear night. They look like stars except they move quite fast in a dead straight line across the sky. You're never gonna spot the geostationary ones though! Learn all the details about satellites, ready for seizing juicy marks.

AQA Syllabus

Section Four — The Earth & Beyond

The Universe

Stars and Solar Systems form from Clouds of Dust

1) Stars form from clouds of dust which spiral in together due to gravitational attraction. 
2) The gravity compresses the matter so much that intense heat develops and sets off nuclear fusion reactions and the star then begins emitting light and other radiation.
3) At the same time that the star is forming, other lumps may develop in the spiralling dust clouds and these eventually gather together and form planets which orbit around the star.

Our Sun is in The Milky Way Galaxy

1) The Sun is one of many millions of stars which form the Milky Way Galaxy.
2) The distance between neighbouring stars is usually millions of times greater than the distance between planets in our Solar System.
   The Milky Way is 100,000 light years across.
3) Gravity is of course the force which keeps the stars together in a galaxy and, like most things in the Universe, the galaxies all rotate, kinda like a catherine wheel only much slower.
4) Our Sun is out towards the end of one of the spiral arms of the Milky Way galaxy.

The Whole Universe has More Than A Billion Galaxies

1) Galaxies themselves are often millions of times further apart than the stars are within a galaxy.
2) So even the slowest amongst you will soon begin to realise that the Universe is mostly empty space and is really really big. Have you ever been to the NEC? Yeah? Well, it's even bigger than that.

Black Holes Don't Let Anything Escape

1) The gravity on neutron stars, white dwarfs and black dwarfs is so strong that it crushes atoms. The stuff in the stars gets squashed up so much that they're MILLIONS OF TIMES DENSER than anything on Earth.
2) If enough matter is left behind after a supernova explosion, it's so dense that nothing can escape the powerful gravitational field. Not even electromagnetic waves. The dead star is then called a black hole. Black holes aren't visible because any light being emitted is sucked right back in there (that's why it's called 'black', d'oh).
3) Astronomers can detect black holes in other ways — they can observe X-rays emitted by hot gases from other stars as they spiral into the black hole.

Galaxies, Milky Way — shove that down yer black hole...

More gripping facts about the Universe. Just look at those numbers: there's millions of stars in the Milky Way and it's 100,000 light years across, the universe contains billions of galaxies, all millions of times further apart than 100,000 light years... Doesn't it just blow your socks off...

Section Four — The Earth & Beyond

The Life Cycle of Stars

The Universe

Stars go through _many traumatic stages_ in their lives — just like teenagers.

Clouds of Dust and Gas

1) Stars _initially form_ from clouds of __DUST AND GAS__.

Protostar

2) The _force of gravity_ makes the dust particles come _spiralling in together_. As they do, _gravitational energy_ is converted into _heat energy_ and the _temperature rises_.

Main Sequence Star

3) When the _temperature_ gets _high enough_, _hydrogen nuclei_ undergo _nuclear fusion_ to form _helium nuclei_ and give out massive amounts of _heat and light_. A star is born. It immediately enters a long _stable period_ where the _heat created_ by the nuclear fusion provides an _outward pressure_ to _BALANCE_ the _force of gravity_ pulling everything _inwards_. In this stable period it's called a __MAIN SEQUENCE STAR__ and it lasts for _billions of years_.
(So the _Earth_ has already had _HALF its innings_ before the Sun _engulfs_ it!)

Red Giant

4) Eventually the _hydrogen_ begins to _run out_ and the star then _swells_ into a __RED GIANT__. It becomes _red_ because the surface _cools_.

5) A __SMALL STAR__ like our Sun will then begin to _cool_ and _contract_ into a __WHITE DWARF__ and then finally, as the light _fades completely_, it becomes a __BLACK DWARF__.
(That's going to be really sad.)

Small stars → White Dwarf → Black Dwarf

Big stars

6) __BIG STARS__ however, start to _glow brightly again_ as they undergo more _fusion_ and _expand and contract several times_ forming _heavier elements_ in various _nuclear reactions_. Eventually they _explode_ in a __SUPERNOVA__.

Supernova

new planetary nebula... ...and a new solar system

Neutron Star... ...or Black Hole

7) The _exploding supernova_ throws the outer layers of _dust and gas_ into space leaving a _very dense core_ called a __NEUTRON STAR__. If the star is _big enough_ this will become a __BLACK HOLE__.

8) The _dust and gas_ thrown off by the supernova may form into __SECOND GENERATION STARS__ like our Sun. The _heavier elements_ are _only_ made in the _final stages_ of a _big star_ or in the final _supernova_, so the _presence_ of heavier elements in the _Sun_ and the _inner planets_ is _clear evidence_ that our beautiful and wonderful world, with its warm sunsets and fresh morning dews, has all formed out of the snotty remains of a grisly old star's last dying sneeze.

9) The _matter_ from which _neutron stars_ and _white dwarfs_ and _black dwarfs_ are made is _MILLIONS OF TIMES DENSER_ than any matter on Earth because the _gravity is so strong_ it even crushes the _atoms_.

Twinkle Twinkle little star, How I wond.. — JUST LEARN IT PAL...

Erm. Just how do they know all that? As if it's not outrageous enough that they reckon to know the whole history of the Earth for the last five billion years, they also reckon to know the whole life cycle of stars, when they're all billions and billions of km away. It's just an outrage.

AQA Syllabus

Section Four — The Earth & Beyond

Searching for Life on Other Planets

The Universe

There's a good chance that life exists somewhere else in the Universe.
Scientists use three methods to search for anything from amoebas to little green men.

1) SETI Looks for Radio Signals from Other Planets

1) Us Earthlings are constantly beaming radio, TV and radar into space for any passing aliens to detect. There might be life out there that's as clever as we are. Or even more clever. They may have built transmitters to send out signals like ours.

2) SETI stands for "Search for Extra Terrestrial Intelligence". Scientists on the SETI project are looking for narrow bands of radio wavelengths coming to Earth from outer space. They're looking for meaningful signals in all the 'noise'.

3) Signals on a narrow band can only come from a transmitter. The 'noise' comes from giant stars and gas clouds.

4) It takes ages to analyse all the radio waves so the SETI folk get help from the public — you can download a screen saver off the internet which analyses a chunk of radio waves.

5) SETI has been going for the last 40 years but they've not found anything. Not a sausage. ☹

6) Scientists are now looking for possible laser signals from outer space. Watch this space...

2) Robots Collect Photos and Samples

1) Scientists have sent robots in spacecrafts to Mars and Europa (one of Jupiter's moons) to look for microorganisms.

2) The robots wander round the planet, sending photographs back to Earth or collecting samples for analysis.

3) Scientists can detect living things or evidence of them, such as fossils or remains, in the samples. This "fossil" is from Mars, though no one really seems sure *what* it is.

4) OK, so a couple of bacteria is a bit boring but that's how we started out on Earth...

3) Chemical Changes and Reflected Light Are Big Clues

Changes Show There's Life

1) Scientists are looking for chemical changes in the atmospheres of other planets.

2) Some changes are just caused by things like volcanoes but others are a clue that there's life there.

3) The amounts of oxygen and carbon dioxide in Earth's atmosphere have changed over time — it's very different to what it'd be like if there was no life here. Plants have made oxygen levels go up but carbon dioxide levels go down.

4) They look at planet's atmospheres from Earth — no spacecraft required.

Light Gives Away What's On The Surface

A planet's reflected light (from the Sun) is different depending on whether it's bounced off rock, trees, water or whatever. It's a good way to find out what's on the surface of a planet.

Scientists haven't found anything exciting (surprise surprise) but they are using these methods to search for planets with suitable conditions for life.

I've got SETI — it's great for watching telly on...

You need to learn these three different ways that scientists are looking for life on other planets. You definitely need to learn this stuff, even if you get given more information in the exam. Cover the page and write notes about how the methods work and what they've found.

Section Four — The Earth & Beyond   *AQA Syllabus*

The Origin of the Universe

The Universe

The *Big Bang Theory* of the Universe is the most *convincing* at the present time. There is also the *steady state theory* which is quite presentable but it *doesn't explain* some of the observed features too well.

Red-shift needs Explaining

There are TWO important bits of evidence you need to know about:

1) Light From Other Galaxies is Red-Shifted

1) When we look at *light* from distant *galaxies* we find that *all the frequencies* are *shifted* towards the *red end* of the spectrum.
2) In other words the *frequencies* are all *slightly lower* than they should be. It's the same effect as a car *horn* sounding lower-pitched when the car is travelling *away* from you. The sound *drops in frequency*.
3) This is called the *Doppler effect*.
4) *Measurements* of the red-shift suggest that *all* the galaxies are *moving away from us* very quickly — and it's the *same result* whichever direction you look in.

2) The Further Away a Galaxy is, The Greater The Red-Shift

1) *More distant galaxies* have *greater* red-shifts than nearer ones.
2) This means that more distant galaxies are *moving away faster* than nearer ones.
3) The *inescapable conclusion* appears to be that the whole Universe is *expanding*.

The Steady State Theory of the Universe — Not Popular

1) This is based on the idea that the Universe appears pretty much *the same everywhere* and *always has done*.
2) In other words the Universe has *always existed* and *always will* in the same form that it is now.
3) This theory explains the *apparent expansion* of the Universe by suggesting that *matter* is being *created* in the spaces as the Universe expands.
4) However, as yet, there's no convincing *explanation* of *where* this new matter *comes from*.
5) There isn't much support for the steady state theory, especially since the discovery of *background radiation* which fits in *much better* with the idea of a Big Bang.
6) But you *just never know*...

Red Shift — it's all in black and white before you...

The steady state theory at the bottom of the page doesn't hold much water, but be aware of it. The thing to learn here is the importance of *red shift*. Seven little points to *learn*, *cover* and *jot down*, then on your lunch-break you can ponder the mysteries of the universe over sarnies.

AQA Syllabus

Section Four — The Earth & Beyond

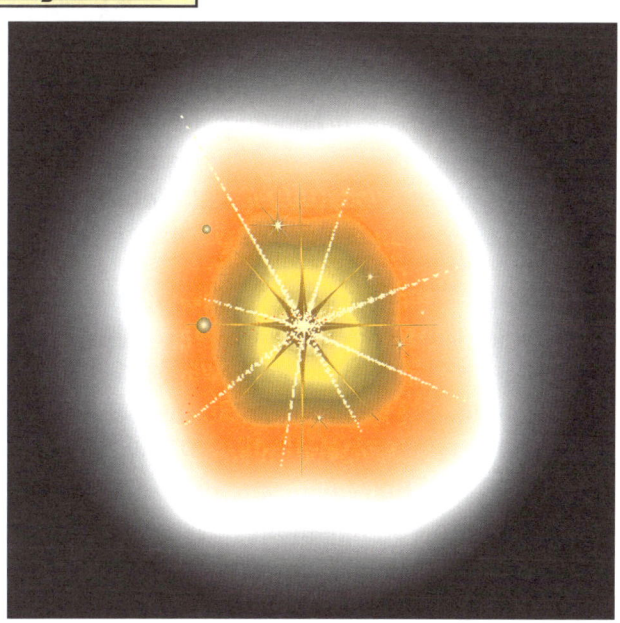

The Future of the Universe

The Universe

The Big Bang Theory — Well Popular

1) Since all the galaxies appear to be _moving apart_ very rapidly, the obvious _conclusion_ is that there was an _initial explosion_: the _Big Bang_.
2) All the matter in the Universe must have been _compressed_ into a _very small space_ and then it _exploded_ and the _expansion_ is still going on.
3) The Big Bang is believed to have happened around _15 billion years ago_.
4) The age of the Universe can be _estimated_ from the current rate of _expansion_.
5) These estimates are _not very accurate_ because it's hard to tell how much the expansion has _slowed down_ since the Big Bang.
6) The rate at which the expansion is _slowing down_ is an _important factor_ in deciding the _future_ of the Universe.
7) _Without gravity_ the Universe would expand at the _same rate forever_.
8) However, the _attraction_ between all the mass in the Universe tends to _slow_ the expansion down.

The Future of the Universe:

It Could Expand Forever — or Collapse into The Big Crunch

1) The eventual fate of the Universe depends on _how fast the galaxies are moving apart_ and how much _total mass_ there is in it.
2) We can _measure_ how fast the galaxies are _separating_ quite easily, but we'd also like to know just _how much mass_ there is in the Universe in order to _predict the future_ of it.
3) This is proving _tricky_ as most of the mass appears to be _invisible_, e.g. _black holes_, _big planets_, _interstellar dust_ etc.

Anyway, depending on how much mass there is, there are _two ways_ the Universe could go:

1) Le Crunch — But Only if there's Enough Mass

If there's _enough mass_ compared to _how fast_ the galaxies are currently moving, the Universe will eventually _stop expanding_ and _begin contracting_. This would end in a _Big Crunch_. The Big Crunch could be followed by another Big Bang and then _endless cycles_ of _expansion and contraction_.

2) If there's Too Little Mass — then it's Le Miserable Eternity

If there's _too little mass_ in the Universe to slow the expansion down, then it could _expand forever_ with the Universe becoming _more and more spread out_ into eternity. This seems _way too dismal_ for my liking. I much prefer the idea of the Universe going _endlessly in cycles_. But what was there _before_ the Universe? Or what is there _outside_ of it? It's _mindboggling_.

Time and Space — it's funny old stuff isn't it...

I think it's great that they've put all this stuff on space in the syllabus. I mean wow, something in Physics that's actually interesting. The great thing about learning a few bits and bobs about the Universe is that it can make you sound really clever when you tell people about it. "Ah well, it's all to do with the diminishing Doppler red-shift over the last 15 billion years", you can say.

Revision Summary for Section Four

The Universe is completely mindblowing. But surely the most mindblowing thing of all is the fact that we're actually here, contemplating the improbability of our own existence. If your mind isn't blowing, then it hasn't sunk in yet. Think about it. 15 billion years ago there was a huge explosion, which set up a whole chain of events that allowed intelligent life to evolve and develop to the point where it became conscious of its own existence. Maaaan — is that freaky or what? The Universe could easily have existed without conscious life ever evolving. Or come to that, the Universe needn't exist at all. Just nothingness. So why does it exist? And why are we here? And why do we have so much revision? Who knows — but stop dreaming and get on with it.

1) Sketch a diagram to explain how day and night come about.
2) Which parts of the world have the longest days and which parts have the shortest days?
3) Sketch a diagram to show how the seasons come about.
4) How long does a full rotation of the Earth take? How long does a full orbit of the Sun take?
5) Which is the biggest planet? Which is the smallest? Sketch the relative sizes of all of them.
6) What is it that keeps the planets in their orbits? What other things are held in orbits?
7) What are constellations? What do planets do in the constellations?
8) Who had trouble with the boys in the red robes? Why did he have such trouble?
9) Describe the differences between the old fashioned view of the Solar System and the one we have now.
10) List the eleven parts of the Solar System starting with the Sun, and get them in the right order.
11) What do planets look like in the night sky?
12) What's the big difference between planets and stars?
13) How does the Sun produce all its heat? What does the Sun give out?
14) What are natural and artificial satellites? Name two natural satellites you can see at night.
15) What four purposes do we have for satellites?
16) Explain fully what a geostationary satellite does, and state what they're used for.
17) Explain fully what a low polar orbit satellite does, and state what they're used for.
18) Which of the two types of satellite takes longer to orbit the Earth? Explain why.
19) What is the Hubble telescope and where is it? What's the big idea there then?
20) What and where are comets? What are they made of? Sketch a diagram of a comet orbit.
21) What do stars and solar systems form from? What force causes it all to happen?
22) How do planets come about? How do you think our solar system was formed?
23) What is the Milky Way? Sketch it and show our Sun in relation to it.
24) How many galaxies is the Universe made up of?
25) Describe the first stages of a star's formation. Where does the initial energy come from?
26) What process eventually starts inside the star to make it produce so much heat and light?
27) What is a "main sequence" star? How long does it last? What's the next stage?
28) What are the final two stages of a small star's life?
29) What are the two final stages of a big star's life?
30) What is meant by a "second generation" star? How do we know our Sun is one?
31) What are the three ways that scientists look for life on other planets?
32) What does SETI stand for?
33) What are the two main theories for the origin of the Universe? Which one is most likely?
34) What are the two important bits of evidence which need explaining by these theories?
35) Give brief details of both theories. How long ago did each suggest the Universe began?
36) What are the two possible futures for the Universe?
37) What do these possible futures depend upon?
38) How strange is the Universe? What's the most mindblowing thing ever?

AQA Syllabus

Section Four — The Earth & Beyond

Energy Resources & Energy Transfer

Energy Transfer

Thermal Energy Transfer

Learn all The Ten Types Of Energy

You should know all of these *well enough* to list them *from memory*, including the examples:

1) **ELECTRICAL** ENERGY............................. — whenever a *current* flows.
2) **LIGHT** ENERGY.................................... — from the *Sun*, *light bulbs* etc.
3) **SOUND** ENERGY................................... — from *loudspeakers* or anything *noisy*.
4) **KINETIC** ENERGY, or **MOVEMENT** ENERGY.... — anything that's *moving* has it.
5) **NUCLEAR** ENERGY................................ — released only from *nuclear reactions*.
6) **THERMAL** ENERGY or **HEAT** ENERGY............ — *flows* from *hot objects* to colder ones.
7) **RADIANT HEAT** ENERGY, or **INFRARED** HEAT — given out as *EM radiation* by *hot objects*.
8) **GRAVITATIONAL POTENTIAL** ENERGY.......... — possessed by anything which can *fall*.
9) **ELASTIC POTENTIAL** ENERGY.................... — stretched *springs*, *elastic*, *rubber bands*, etc.
10) **CHEMICAL** ENERGY.............................. — possessed by *foods*, *fuels* and *batteries*.

Potential- and Chemical- are forms of Stored Energy

The *last three* above are forms of *stored energy* because the energy is not obviously *doing* anything, it's kind of *waiting to happen*, i.e. waiting to be turned into one of the *other* forms.

They Like Giving Exam Questions on Energy Transfers

These are *very important examples*. You must *learn them* till you can repeat them all *easily*.

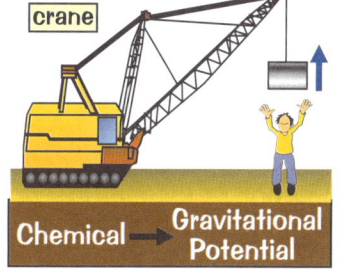

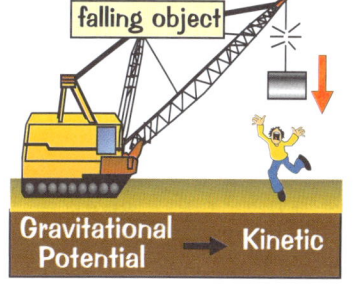

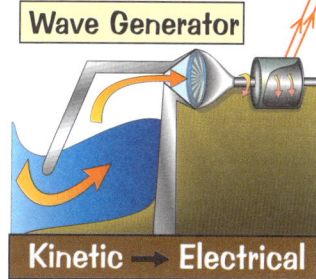

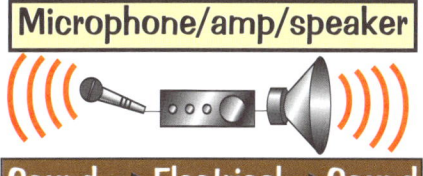

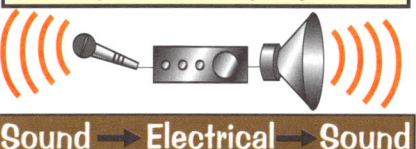

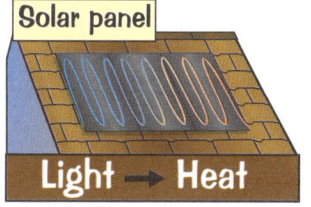

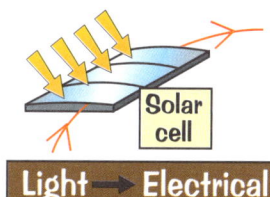

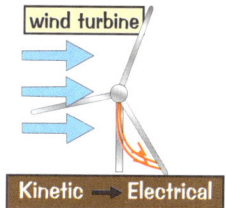

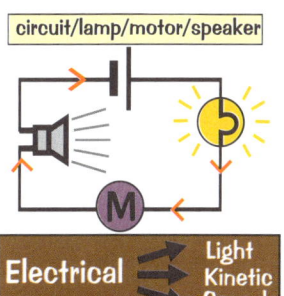

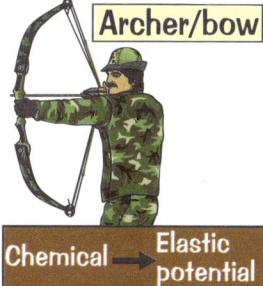

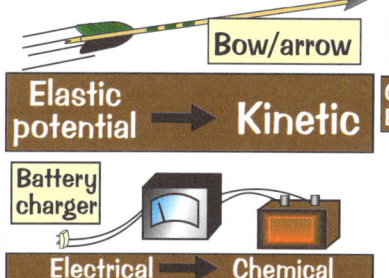

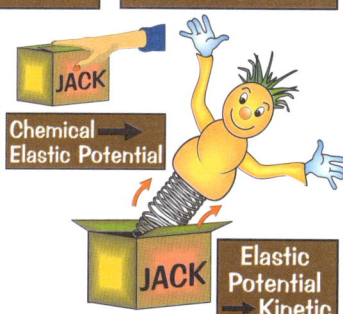

Eating food / respiration: Chemical → Heat, kinetic, chemical

crane: Chemical → Gravitational Potential

falling object: Gravitational Potential → Kinetic

Wave Generator: Kinetic → Electrical

Microphone/amp/speaker: Sound → Electrical → Sound

Solar panel: Light → Heat

Solar cell: Light → Electrical

wind turbine: Kinetic → Electrical

circuit/lamp/motor/speaker: Electrical → Light, Kinetic, Sound

Archer/bow: Chemical → Elastic potential

Bow/arrow: Elastic potential → Kinetic

Battery charger: Electrical → Chemical

JACK: Chemical → Elastic Potential; Elastic Potential → Kinetic

And DON'T FORGET — ALL types of ENERGY are measured in JOULES

Learn about Energy — and just keep working at it...

They're pretty keen on the different types of energy and also energy transfers. You'll definitely get an Exam question on it, and if you learn all the stuff on this page, you should have it pretty well covered I'd think. *Learn, cover, scribble, check, learn, cover, scribble*, etc. etc.

Section Five — Energy Resources & Energy Transfer — AQA Syllabus

Heat Transfer

Thermal Energy Transfer

There are *three* distinct methods of heat transfer: *CONDUCTION*, *CONVECTION* and *RADIATION*.
To answer Exam questions you *must* use those *three key words* in just the *right places*.
And that means you need to know *exactly what they are*, and all the *differences* between them.

Heat Energy Causes Molecules to Move Faster

1) *Heat energy* causes *gas and liquid* molecules to move around *faster*, and causes particles in solids to vibrate *more rapidly*.
2) When particles move *faster* it shows up as a *rise* in temperature.
3) This extra *kinetic energy* in the particles tends to get *dissipated* to the *surroundings*.
4) In other words the *heat* energy tends to flow *away* from a hotter object to its *cooler* surroundings. But then you knew that already. I would hope.

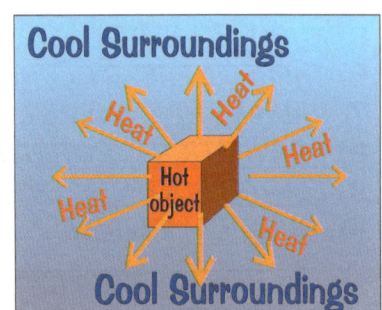

> If there's a *DIFFERENCE IN TEMPERATURE* between two places then *HEAT WILL FLOW* between them.

Conduction, Convection and Radiation Compared

These differences are really important — make sure you *LEARN them*:

1) *Conduction* occurs mainly in *solids*.
2) *Convection* occurs mainly in *gases and liquids*.
3) Gases and liquids are *very poor conductors* — convection is usually the *dominant* process. Where convection *can't* occur, the heat transfer by *conduction* is *very slow* indeed:
4) *Radiation* travels through anything *see-through* including a *vacuum*.
5) *Heat Radiation* is given out by *anything* which is *warm or hot*.
6) The *amount* of heat radiation which is *absorbed or emitted* depends on the *colour* and *texture* of the *surface*.
   But don't forget, *convection* and *conduction* are totally *unaffected* by surface colour or texture. A *shiny white* surface *conducts* just as well as a *matt black* one.

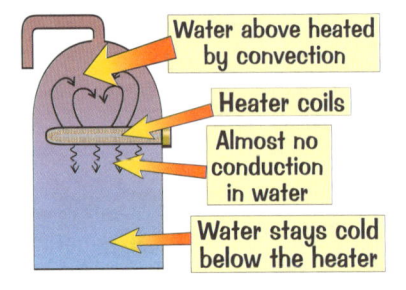

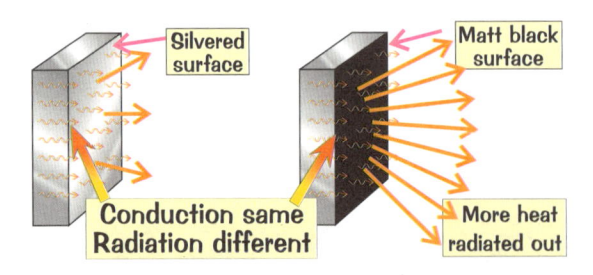

Water above heated by convection
Heater coils
Almost no conduction in water
Water stays cold below the heater

Silvered surface
Matt black surface
Conduction same Radiation different
More heat radiated out

Learn the facts on heat transfer — but don't get a sweat on...

Phew, no more numbers and formulae, now we're back to good old straightforward factual learning again. Much less confusing — but no less of a challenge, it has to be said. You've really got to make a fair old effort to get those three key processes of heat transfer all sorted out in your head so that you know exactly what they are and when they occur. *Learn and grin*.

AQA Syllabus — Section Five — Energy Resources & Energy Transfer

Conduction of Heat

Thermal Energy Transfer

Conduction of Heat — Occurs Mainly in Solids

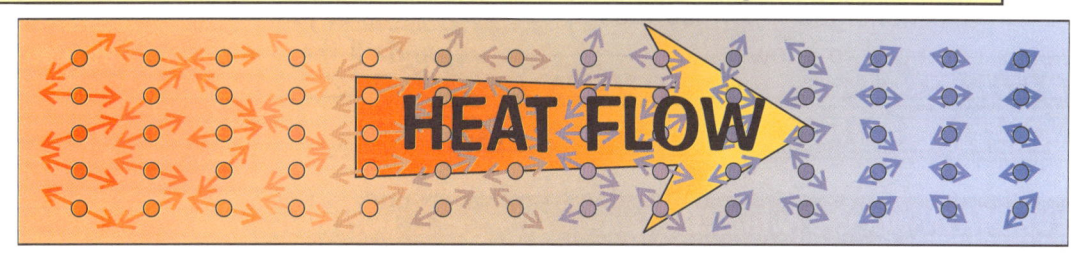

HOT — HEAT FLOW — **COLD**

CONDUCTION OF HEAT is the process where VIBRATING PARTICLES pass on their EXTRA VIBRATION ENERGY to NEIGHBOURING PARTICLES.

This process continues *throughout the solid* and gradually the *extra vibrational energy* (or *heat*) is passed all the way through the solid, causing a *rise in temperature* at the other side.

Non-metals are Good Insulators

1) This normal process of *conduction* as illustrated above is always *very slow*.
2) But in most *non-metal solids* it's the *only* way that heat can pass through.
3) So *non-metals*, such as *plastic*, *wood*, *rubber* etc. are very good *insulators*.
4) Non-metal *gases and liquids* are even *worse conductors*, as you will slowly begin to realise if I say it often enough. Metals, on the other hand, are a totally different ball game...

All Metals Are Good Conductors due to their Free Electrons

HOT — Heat carried in metals by the free electrons — **COLD**

Higher Higher Higher ... *Higher Higher Higher*

1) *Metals* "*conduct*" so well because the electrons are *free to move* inside the metal.
2) At the *hot end* the electrons move *faster* and diffuse *more quickly* through the metal.
3) So the electrons carry their *energy* quite a *long way* before *giving it up* in a *collision*.
4) This is obviously a much *faster way* of *transferring* the energy through the metal than slowly passing it between jostling *neighbouring* atoms. This is why *heat* travels so *fast* through *metals*.

Metals always FEEL hotter or colder because they conduct so well

You'll notice if a *spade* is left out in the *sun* that the *metal part* will always *feel* much *hotter* than the *wooden* handle. But *IT ISN'T HOTTER* — it just *conducts* the heat into your hand much quicker than the wood, so your hand *heats up* much quicker.

In *cold weather*, the *metal bits* of a spade, or anything else, always *feel colder* because they *take the heat away* from your hand quicker. But they're *NOT COLDER*... Remember that.

Good conductors are always metals? — what about Henry Wood...

Here's a little joker with which to amaze and entertain your family and friends at Christmas: the only reason metals are such good "conductors" is because the free electrons *convect* the heat through the metal. Is it true? Answers on a post card. *Learn this page* then *cover and scribble*.

SECTION FIVE — Energy Resources & Energy Transfer   *AQA Syllabus*

Convection of Heat

Thermal Energy Transfer

Gases and liquids are usually free to _slosh about_ — and that allows them to transfer heat by _convection_, which is a _much more effective process_ than conduction.

Convection of Heat — Liquids and Gases Only

Convection simply _can't happen in solids_ because the particles _can't move_.

CONVECTION occurs when the more energetic particles _MOVE_ from the _hotter region_ to the _cooler region_ — AND TAKE THEIR HEAT ENERGY WITH THEM

When the _more energetic_ (i.e. _hotter_) particles get somewhere _cooler_ they then _transfer their energy_ by the usual process of _collisions_ which warm up the surroundings.

Natural Convection Currents Are Caused By Changes in Density

The diagram shows a _typical convection current_. Make sure you _learn_ all the bits about _expansion_ and _density changes_ which _cause_ the convection current. It's all worth _juicy marks_ in the Exam.

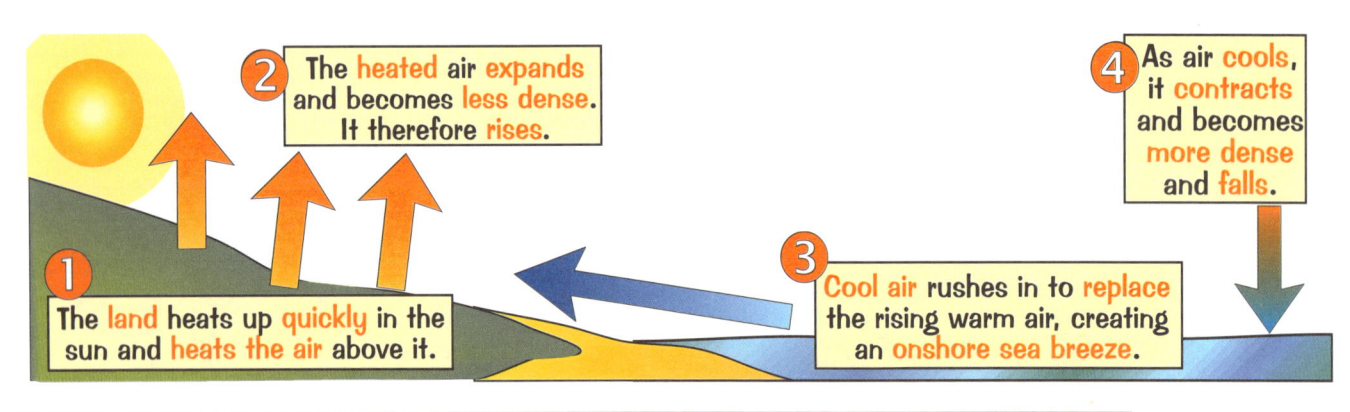

① The land heats up quickly in the sun and heats the air above it.

② The heated air expands and becomes less dense. It therefore rises.

③ Cool air rushes in to replace the rising warm air, creating an onshore sea breeze.

④ As air cools, it contracts and becomes more dense and falls.

Forced Convection is Used to Cool Machinery and Us

1) _Forced convection_ is simply where you have a _fan_ or _pump_ making the gas or liquid move around _much faster_.

2) In a _car engine_ the _water pump_ pushes the water around quickly to _transfer heat_ away from the _engine_ and get rid of it at the _radiator_. That's _forced convection_.

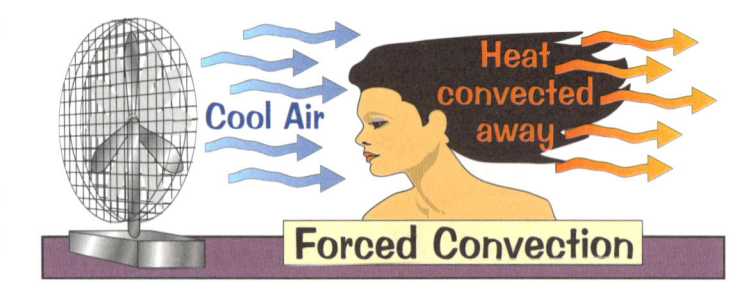

3) Inside, we use _cooling fans_ to blow air over us to _cool us down_, or alternatively _fan heaters_ blow warm air around the room _much quicker_ than the natural convection currents would.

Convection Currents — easy as a summer evening breeze...

Oi! Watch out! It's another pair of Physics words that look so much alike that half of you think they're the same word. Look: CONVECTION. See, it's different from CONDUCTION. Tricky that one isn't it. Just like reflection and refraction. Not just a different word though, convection is a _totally different process_ too. Make sure you learn exactly why it isn't like conduction.

Heat Radiation

Thermal Energy Transfer

Heat radiation can also be called *infrared radiation*, and it consists purely of electromagnetic waves of a certain frequency. It's just below visible light in the *electromagnetic spectrum*.

Heat Radiation Can Travel Through Vacuum

Heat radiation is *different* from the other *two methods* of heat transfer in quite a few ways:
1) It travels in *straight lines* at the *speed of light*.
2) It travels through *vacuum*. This is the *only way* that heat can reach us *from the Sun*.
3) It can be very effectively *reflected* away again by a *silver* surface.
4) It only travels through *transparent* media, like *air*, *glass* and *water*.
5) Its behaviour is strongly *dependent* on *surface colour and texture*. This *definitely isn't so* for conduction and convection.
6) No *particles* are involved. It's *transfer* of *heat* energy purely by *waves*.

Emission and Absorption of Heat Radiation

1) *All objects* are *continually* emitting and absorbing *heat radiation*.
2) The *hotter* they are the *more* heat radiation they *emit*.
3) *Cooler ones* around them will *absorb* this heat radiation. You can *feel* this *heat radiation* if you stand near something *hot* like a fire.

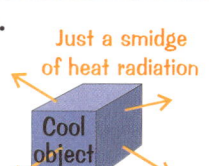

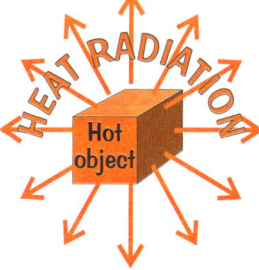

It Depends An Awful Lot on Surface Colour and Texture

1) *Dark matt* surfaces ABSORB heat radiation falling on them much more *strongly* than *bright glossy* surfaces, such as *gloss white* or *silver*. They also *emit* heat radiation *much more* too.
2) *Silvered* surfaces REFLECT nearly all heat radiation falling on them.
3) In the lab there are several fairly dull experiments to demonstrate *the effects of surface* on *emission and absorption* of heat radiation. Here are two of the most gripping:

Leslie's Cube

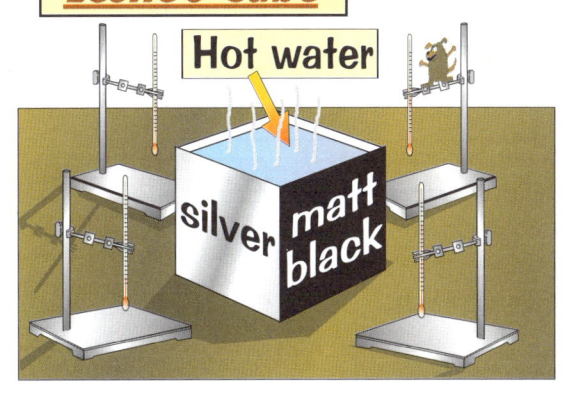

The *matt black* side EMITS most heat so its that thermometer which gets *hottest*.

The *matt black* surface ABSORBS *most heat* so its wax *melts* first and the ball bearing *drops*.

The Melting Wax Trick

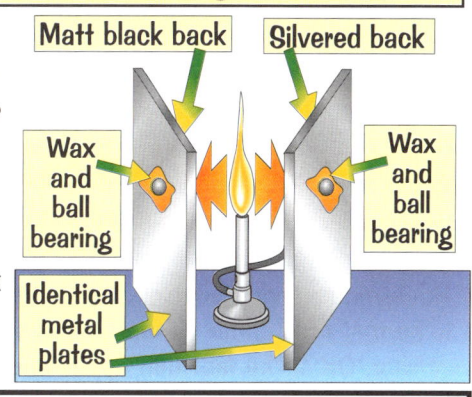

Revise Heat Radiation — absorb as much as you can, anyway...

The main thing to learn here is that heat radiation is strongly affected by the colour and texture of surfaces. Don't forget that the other two types of heat transfer, conduction and convection, are not affected by surface colour and texture *at all*. Heat radiation is totally different from conduction and convection. *Learn* all the details on this page, then *cover it up* and *scribble*.

Section Five — Energy Resources & Energy Transfer — AQA Syllabus

Applications of Heat Transfer

Thermal Energy Transfer

Good Conductors and Good Insulators

1) *All metals* are *good* conductors e.g. iron, brass, aluminium, copper, gold, silver etc.
2) All *non-metals* are good *insulators*.
3) Gases and liquids are truly *abysmal conductors* (but are great *convectors* don't forget).
4) The *best* insulators are ones which trap *pockets of air*. If the air *can't move*, it *can't* transfer heat by *convection* and so the heat has to *conduct* very slowly through the *pockets of air*, as well as the material in between. This really slows it down *big style*.
   This is how *clothes* and *blankets* and *loft insulation* and *cavity wall insulation* and *polystyrene cups* and *pretty woollen mittens* and *little furry animals* and *fluffy yellow ducklings* work.

Insulation should also take account of Heat Radiation

1) *Silvered finishes* are highly effective *insulation* against heat transfer by *radiation*.
2) This can work *both ways*, either keeping heat radiation *out* or keeping heat *in*.

KEEPING HEAT RADIATION OUT:	KEEPING HEAT IN:
Spacesuits	Shiny metal kettles
Cooking foil on the turkey	Survival blankets
Thermos flasks	Thermos flasks (again)

3) *Matt black* is rarely used for its thermal properties of *absorbing* and *emitting* heat radiation.
4) It's only *useful* where you want to *get rid of heat*, e.g. the *cooling fins* or *radiator* on an engine.

The Thermos Flask — The Ultimate in Insulation

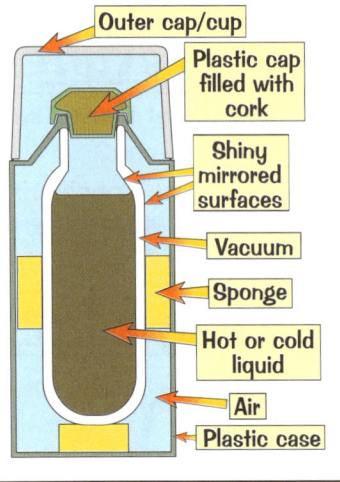

Labels on diagram: Outer cap/cup, Plastic cap filled with cork, Shiny mirrored surfaces, Vacuum, Sponge, Hot or cold liquid, Air, Plastic case

1) The glass bottle is *double-walled* with a *thin vacuum* between the two walls. This stops *all conduction* and *convection* through the *sides*.
2) The walls either side of the vacuum are *silvered* to keep heat loss by *radiation* to a *minimum*.
3) The bottle is supported using *insulating foam*. This minimises heat *conduction* to or from the *outer* glass bottle.
4) The *stopper* is made of *plastic* and filled with *cork or foam* to reduce any *heat conduction* through it.

In *Exam questions* you must *always* say which form of heat transfer is involved at any point, either *conduction*, *convection* or *radiation*.
"*The vacuum stops heat getting out*" will get you *no marks at all*.

Convection Heaters and "Radiators" — Watch out!

1) A "*radiator*" strictly should be something that *glows red* and gives most heat out as *radiation*, like a *coal fire* or an *electric bar radiator*.
2) Central heating "*radiators*" have the *wrong name* really, because they're not like that at all. They give *most* heat out as *convection currents* of warm rising air. This is what a "*convector heater*" does.

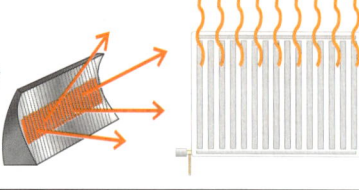

Heat Transfer and Insulation — keep taking it all in...

There's a lot more to insulation than you first realise. That's because there are *three ways* that heat can be transferred, and so effective heat insulation has to deal with *all three*, of course. The venerable Thermos Flask is the classic example of all-in-one-full-blown insulation. *Learn it*.

AQA Syllabus — Section Five — Energy Resources & Energy Transfer

Keeping Buildings Warm

Thermal Energy Transfer

Loft Insulation
Initial Cost: £200
Annual Saving: £50
Payback time: *4 years*

Hot Water Tank Jacket
Initial Cost: £10
Annual Saving: £15
Payback time: *1 year*

Thermostatic Controls
Initial Cost: £100
Annual Saving: £20
Payback time: *5 years*

Double Glazing
Initial Cost: £3,000
Annual Saving: £60
Payback time: *50 years*

Cavity Wall Insulation
Initial Cost: £500
Annual Saving: £70
Payback time: *7 years*

Draught-proofing
Initial Cost: £50
Annual Saving: £50
Payback time: *1 year*

Effectiveness and Cost-effectiveness are not the same...

1) The figures above are all in the right "ball park", but of course it'll *vary* from house to house.
2) The *cheaper* methods of insulation tend to be a *lot* more *cost-effective* than the pricier ones.
3) The ones that save the *most money* each year could be considered the most "*effective*". i.e. *cavity wall insulation*. How *cost-effective* it is depends on what *time-scale* you're looking at.
4) If you *subtract* the *annual saving* from the *initial cost* repeatedly then *eventually* the one with the *biggest annual saving* must always come out as the winner, if you think about it.
5) But you might sell the house (or die) before that happens. If instead you look at it over say, a *five-year period* then the cheap and cheerful *draught-proofing* wins. Who's to say?
6) But *double glazing* is always *by far* the *least cost-effective*, which is kinda comical, considering.

Know Which Types of Heat Transfer are Involved:

1) **CAVITY WALL INSULATION** — foam squirted into the gap between the bricks reduces *convection* and *radiation* across the gap.
2) **LOFT INSULATION** — a thick layer of fibre glass wool laid out across the whole loft floor reduces *conduction* and *radiation* into the roof space from the ceiling.
3) **DRAUGHT PROOFING** — strips of foam and plastic around doors and windows stop draughts of cold air blowing in, i.e. they reduce heat loss due to *convection*.
4) **DOUBLE GLAZING** — two layers of glass with an air gap reduce *conduction* and *radiation*.
5) **THERMOSTATIC RADIATOR VALVES** — these simply prevent the house being *over-warmed*.
6) **HOT WATER TANK JACKET** — lagging such as fibre glass wool reduces *conduction* and *radiation* from the hot water tank.
7) **THICK CURTAINS** — big bits of cloth you pull across the window to stop people looking in at you, but also to reduce heat loss by *conduction* and *radiation*.

They don't seem to have these problems in Spain...

Remember, the most *effective* insulation measure is the one which keeps the most heat in, (biggest annual saving). If your house had no roof, then a roof would be the most *effective* measure, would it not! But *cost-effectiveness* depends very much on the *time-scale* involved.

Section Five — Energy Resources & Energy Transfer — AQA Syllabus

Useful Energy Transfers

Thermal Energy Transfer

Most Energy Transfers Involve Some Losses, as Heat

Energy is ONLY USEFUL when it's CONVERTED from one form to another.

1) <u>Useful devices</u> are only <u>useful</u> because they <u>convert</u> energy from <u>one form</u> to <u>another</u>.
2) In doing so, some of the useful <u>input energy</u> is always <u>lost or wasted</u> as <u>heat</u>.
3) The <u>less energy</u> that is <u>wasted</u>, the <u>more efficient</u> the device is said to be.
4) The energy flow diagram is pretty much the same for <u>all devices</u>. You MUST learn this <u>BASIC ENERGY FLOW DIAGRAM</u>:

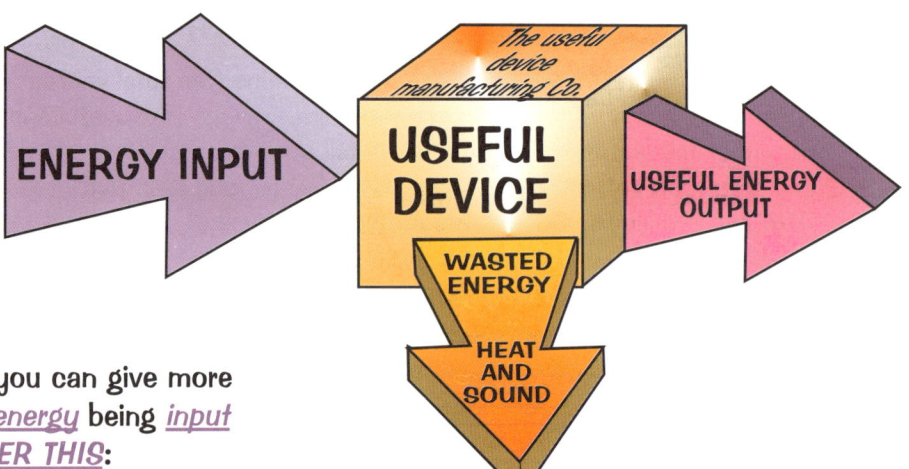

ENERGY INPUT → USEFUL DEVICE → USEFUL ENERGY OUTPUT
                             ↓ WASTED ENERGY — HEAT AND SOUND

For any <u>specific example</u> you can give more detail about the <u>types of energy</u> being <u>input</u> and <u>output</u>, but REMEMBER THIS:

<u>NO</u> device is 100% efficient and the <u>WASTED ENERGY</u> is always <u>dissipated</u> as <u>HEAT</u> and <u>SOUND</u>.

<u>Electric heaters</u> are the <u>exception</u> to this. They're <u>100% efficient</u> because <u>all</u> the electricity is converted to <u>"useful"</u> heat. <u>What else could it become?</u> Ultimately, <u>all</u> energy ends up as <u>heat energy</u>. If you use an electric drill, it gives out <u>various types</u> of energy but they all quickly end up as <u>heat</u>. The wasted energy <u>and</u> the useful energy both end up just <u>warming the air</u> around us. This energy very quickly <u>spreads out</u> into the surroundings and then it becomes harder and harder to make use of it for further energy transfers. That's an important thing to realise. So realise it — and <u>never forget it</u>.

Don't waste energy — Don't switch anything on

Make sure you know all these easy examples — one of them is <u>bound</u> to come up in your Exams.

Device	Energy Input	Useful Output	Wasted Energy
1) Television	Electrical	Light and Sound	Heat
2) Light Bulb	Electrical	Light	Heat
3) Electric Drill	Electrical	Movement	Heat and Sound
4) Hairdryer	Electrical	Heat	Heat and Sound
5) Car Engine	Chemical	Movement	Heat and Sound
6) Horse	Chemical	Movement and ...	Heat and Sound

Learn about energy dissipation — but keep your cool...

The thing about loss of energy is it's always the same — it always disappears as heat and sound, and even the sound ends up as heat pretty quickly. So when they ask "Why is the input energy more than the output energy?", the answer is always the same... <u>Learn and enjoy</u>.

AQA Syllabus   Section Five — Energy Resources & Energy Transfer

Efficiency of Machines

Efficiency

A _machine_ is a device which turns _one type of energy_ into _another_.
The _efficiency_ of any device is defined as:

$$\text{Efficiency} = \frac{\text{USEFUL Energy OUTPUT}}{\text{TOTAL Energy INPUT}}$$

$$\frac{\text{Energy out}}{\text{Efficiency} \times \text{Energy in}}$$

You can give efficiency as a _fraction_, _decimal_ or _percentage_. i.e. ¾ or 0.75 or 75%

Come on! — Efficiency is Really Simple...

1) You find how much energy is _supplied_ to a machine (the total energy INPUT).
2) You find how much _useful energy_ the machine _delivers_ (the useful energy OUTPUT).
   They either tell you this directly or they tell you how much it _wastes_ as heat/sound.
3) Either way, you get those _two important numbers_ and then just _divide_ the _smaller one_ by the _bigger one_ to get a value for _efficiency_ somewhere between _0 and 1_ (or _0 and 100%_). Easy.
4) The other way they might ask it is to tell you the _efficiency_ and the _input energy_ and ask for the _energy output_. The best way to tackle that is to _learn_ this _other version_ of the formula:

USEFUL ENERGY OUTPUT = Efficiency × TOTAL Energy INPUT

Five Important Examples on Efficiency for you to Learn

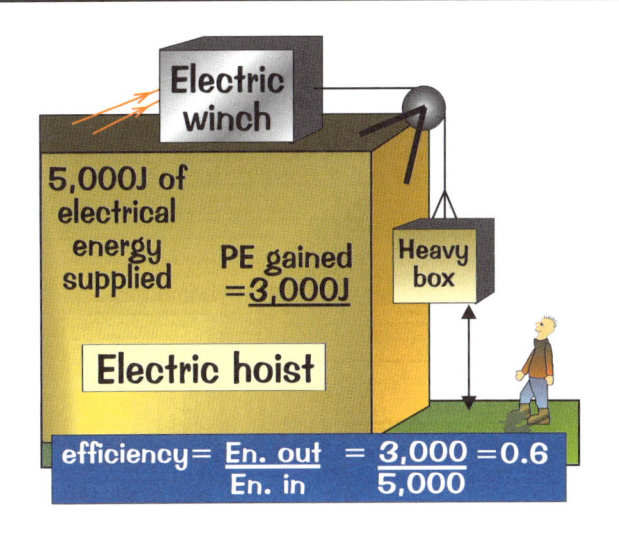

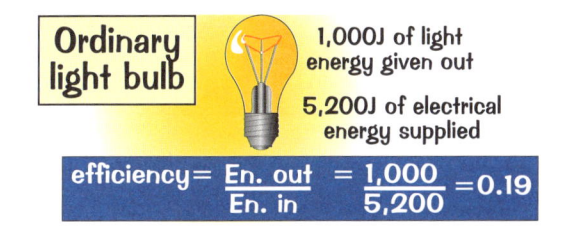

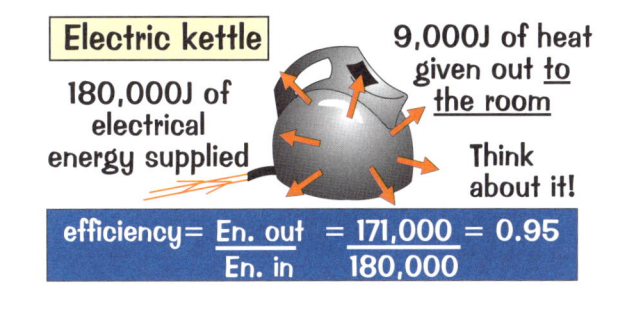

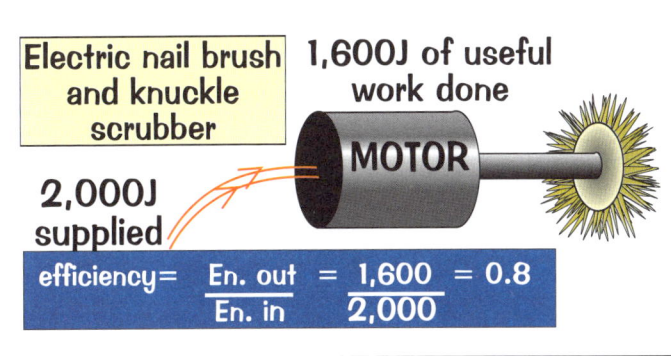

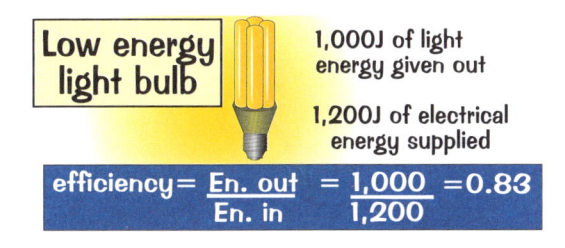

Electric winch / Electric hoist
5,000J of electrical energy supplied
PE gained = 3,000J
Heavy box

efficiency = En. out / En. in = 3,000 / 5,000 = 0.6

Ordinary light bulb
1,000J of light energy given out
5,200J of electrical energy supplied

efficiency = En. out / En. in = 1,000 / 5,200 = 0.19

Electric kettle
180,000J of electrical energy supplied
9,000J of heat given out _to the room_
Think about it!

efficiency = En. out / En. in = 171,000 / 180,000 = 0.95

Electric nail brush and knuckle scrubber
1,600J of useful work done
MOTOR
2,000J supplied

efficiency = En. out / En. in = 1,600 / 2,000 = 0.8

Low energy light bulb
1,000J of light energy given out
1,200J of electrical energy supplied

efficiency = En. out / En. in = 1,000 / 1,200 = 0.83

Learn about energy transfer — but do it efficiently...

Efficiency is another hideously simple concept. It's a big funny-looking word I grant you, but that doesn't mean it's tricky. Let's face it, efficiency's a blummin' doddle — divide E_{out} by E_{in} and there it is, done. Geesh. _Learn the page_, then _cover it up_ and _scribble down_ what you know.

Section Five — Energy Resources & Energy Transfer   AQA Syllabus

Sources of Power

Energy Resources

There are _twelve_ different types of _energy resource_.
They fit into _two broad types_: _RENEWABLE_ and _NON-RENEWABLE_.

Non-renewable Energy Resources Will Run Out One Day

The _non-renewables_ are the _THREE FOSSIL FUELS_ and _NUCLEAR_:

1) _COAL_
2) _OIL_
3) _NATURAL GAS_
4) _NUCLEAR FUELS_ (_uranium_ and _plutonium_)

a) They will _ALL RUN OUT_ one day.
b) They all do _DAMAGE_ to the environment.
c) But they provide _MOST OF OUR ENERGY_.

Renewable Energy Resources Will Never Run Out

The _renewables_ are:

1) _WIND_
2) _WAVES_
3) _TIDES_
4) _HYDROELECTRIC_
5) _SOLAR_
6) _GEOTHERMAL_
7) _FOOD_
8) _BIOMASS (WOOD)_

a) These will _NEVER RUN OUT_.
b) They _DO NOT DAMAGE THE ENVIRONMENT_ (except visually).
c) The trouble is they _DON'T PROVIDE MUCH ENERGY_ and many of them are _UNRELIABLE_ because they depend on the _WEATHER_.

Comparison of Renewables and Non-Renewables

1) They're quite likely to give you an Exam question asking you to "_evaluate_" or "_discuss_" the _relative merits_ of generating power by _renewable_ and _non-renewable_ resources.
2) The way to _get the marks_ is to simply list the _pros and cons_ of each method.
3) Full details are given on the next few pages. However there are some _clear generalisations_ you should _definitely learn_ to help you answer such questions. Make sure you can _list these easily from memory_:

Non-Renewable Resources (Coal, Oil, Gas and Nuclear):

ADVANTAGES:
1) _High_ output.
2) _Reliable_ output.
3) They don't take up much _land_.
4) They can _match demand_ for power.

DISADVANTAGES:
1) Very _polluting_.
2) They involve _mining or drilling_, and then _transportation_ of fuels.
3) They are _running out_ quite quickly.
4) High cost of _building and de-commissioning_ of power stations.

Renewable Resources (Wind, Waves, Solar etc.):

ADVANTAGES:
1) _No pollution_.
2) _No fuel costs_.
   (although the initial costs are high).

DISADVANTAGES:
1) Require _large areas of land_ or water and often _spoil the landscape_.
2) They don't always deliver _when needed_ — if the weather isn't right, for example.

Stop fuelling around and learn this stuff properly...

There's a lot of details here on sources of energy — an awful lot of details. Trouble is, in the Exam they could test you on any of them, so I guess you just gotta learn 'em.

Power from Non-Renewables

Energy Resources

Most of the electricity we use is generated from the four NON-RENEWABLE sources of energy (coal, oil, gas and nuclear) in big power stations, which are all pretty much the same apart from the boiler. Learn the basic features of the typical power station shown here and also the nuclear reactor.

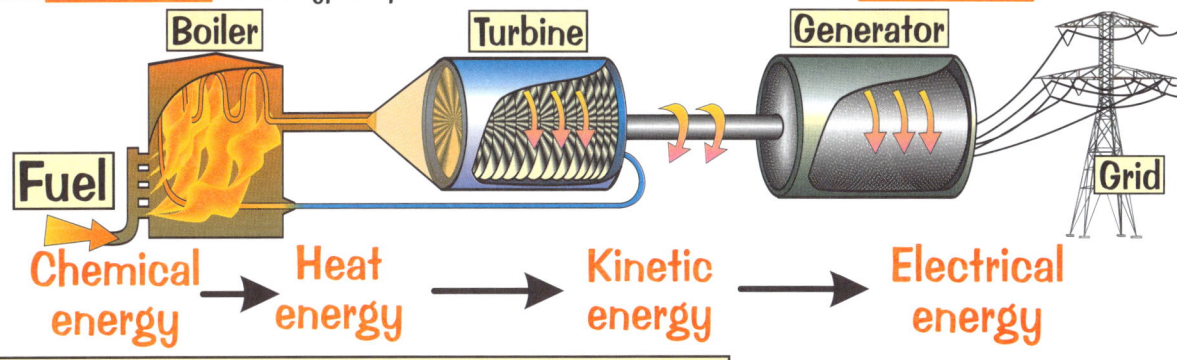

Fuel → Boiler → Turbine → Generator → Grid

Chemical energy → Heat energy → Kinetic energy → Electrical energy

Nuclear Reactors are Just Fancy Boilers

1) A nuclear power station is mostly the same as the one shown above, where heat is produced in a boiler to make steam to drive turbines etc. The difference is in the boiler, as shown here:
2) They take the longest time of all the non-renewables to start up. Natural gas takes the shortest time.

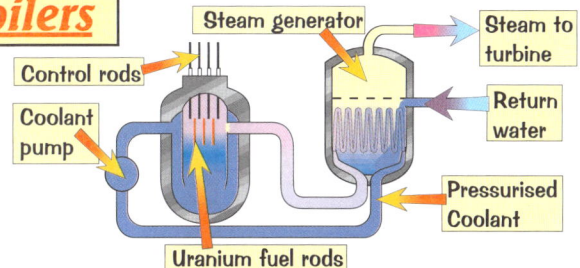

(Diagram labels: Steam generator, Steam to turbine, Control rods, Return water, Coolant pump, Pressurised Coolant, Uranium fuel rods)

Environmental Problems with the use of Non-Renewables

1) All three fossil fuels, (coal, oil and gas) release CO_2. For the same amount of energy produced, coal releases the most CO_2, followed by oil then gas. All this CO_2 adds to the Greenhouse Effect, causing global warming. There's no feasible way to stop it being released either. Ho hum.
2) Burning coal and oil releases sulphur dioxide which causes acid rain. This is reduced by taking the sulphur out before it's burned or cleaning up the emissions.
3) Coal mining makes a mess of the landscape, especially 'open-cast mining'.
4) Oil spillages cause serious environmental problems. We try to avoid it, but it'll always happen.
5) Nuclear power is clean but the nuclear waste is very dangerous and difficult to dispose of.
6) Nuclear fuel (i.e. uranium) is cheap but the overall cost of nuclear power is high due to the cost of the power plant and final de-commissioning.
7) Nuclear power always carries the risk of major catastrophe like the Chernobyl disaster.

The Non-Renewables Need to be Conserved

1) When the fossil fuels eventually run out we will have to use other forms of energy.
2) More importantly however, fossil fuels (especially crude oil) are also a very useful source of chemicals, which will be hard to replace when they are all gone.
3) To stop the fossil fuels running out so quickly there are two things we can do:

1) Use Less Energy by Being More Efficient with it:
(i) Better insulation of buildings,
(ii) Turning lights and other things off when not needed,
(iii) Making everyone drive spiddly little cars with little engines.

2) Use More of the Renewable Sources of Energy
as detailed on the following pages.

Learn about the non-renewables — before it's too late...

Make sure you realise that we generate most of our electricity from the four non-renewables, and that the power stations are all pretty much the same, as exemplified by the above diagram. Also make sure you know all the problems about them and why we should use less of them.

Section Five — Energy Resources & Energy Transfer   *AQA Syllabus*

Power from Renewables

Energy Resources

Wind Power — Lots of Little Wind Turbines

1) This involves putting lots of windmills (wind turbines) up in exposed places like on moors or round coasts.
2) Each wind turbine has its own generator inside it so the electricity is generated directly from the wind turning the blades, which turn the generator. There's no pollution.
3) But they do spoil the view. You need about 5000 wind turbines to replace one coal-fired power station and 5000 of them cover a lot of ground — that wouldn't look very nice at all.
4) There's also the problem of no power when the wind stops, and it's impossible to increase supply when there's extra demand.

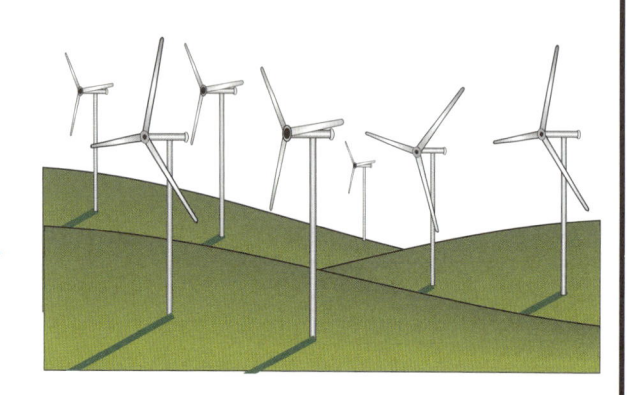

Hydroelectricity — Flooding Valleys

1) Hydroelectric power usually requires the flooding of a valley by building a big dam.
2) Rainwater is caught and allowed out through turbines. There is no pollution.
3) There is quite a big impact on the environment due to the flooding of the valley and possible loss of habitat for some species.
4) A big advantage is immediate response to increased demand and there's no problem with reliability except in times of drought.

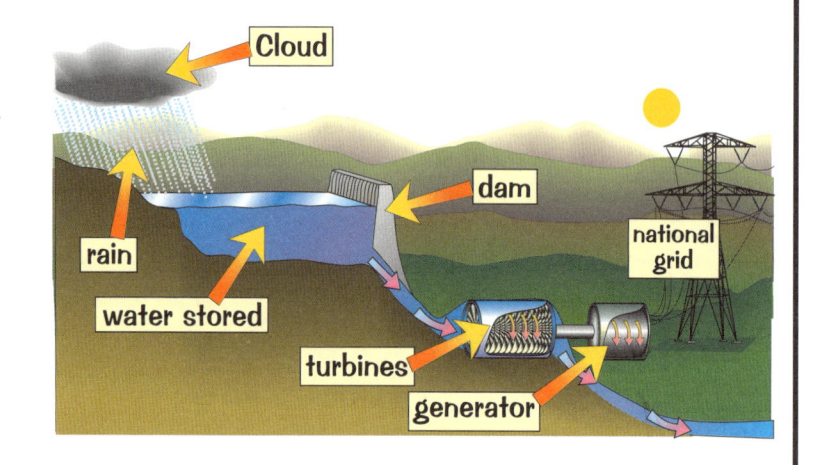

Wood Burning — Environmentally OK

1) It involves the cultivation of fast-growing trees which are then harvested, chopped up and burnt in a power station furnace to produce electricity.

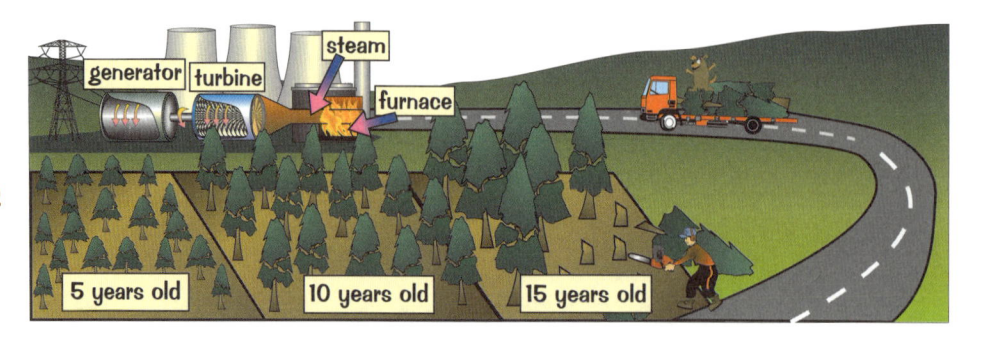

2) The trees are grown as quickly as they are burnt so they will never run out. This does not apply to the burning of rainforests where the trees take much longer to grow.

Learn about Wind Power — it can blow your mind...

Lots of important details here on these nice green squeaky clean sources of energy — pity they make such a mess of the landscape. Three nice green squeaky clean mini-essays please.

AQA Syllabus — *Section Five — Energy Resources & Energy Transfer*

Power from Renewables

Energy Resources

Wave Power — Lots of little Wave Converters

1) You need lots of small generators located around the coast.
2) As waves come in to the shore they provide an up and down motion which can be used to drive a generator.
3) They are fairly unreliable, since waves tend to die out when the wind drops.
4) The main environmental problem is spoiling the view.

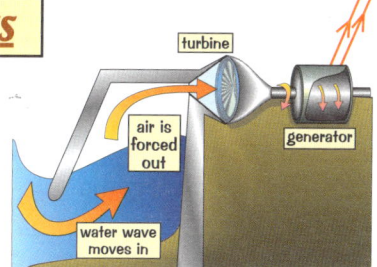

Tidal Barrages — Using The Sun and Moon's Gravity

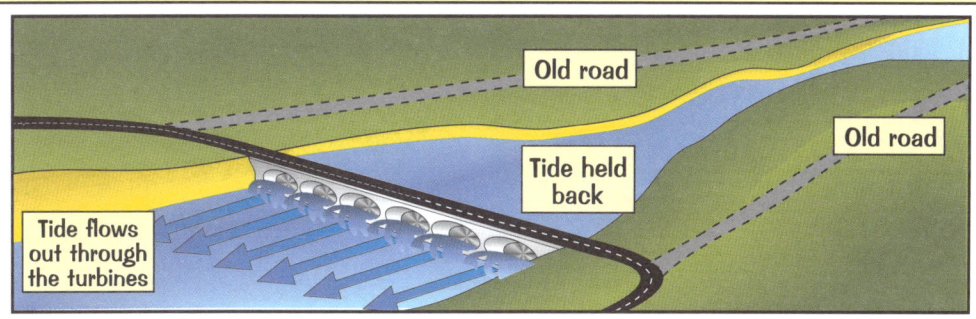

1) Tidal barrages are big dams built across river estuaries with turbines in them.
2) As the tide comes in it fills up the estuary to a height of several metres. This water can then be allowed out through turbines at a controlled speed. It also drives the turbines on the way in.
3) The main problems are preventing free access by boats, spoiling the view and altering the habitat of the wildlife eg: wading birds, sea creatures and beasties who live in the sand.
4) Tides are pretty reliable in the sense that they happen twice a day without fail, and always to the predicted height. The only drawback is that the height of the tide is variable so lower (neap) tides will provide significantly less energy than the bigger spring tides. But tidal barrages are excellent for storing energy ready for periods of peak demand.

Solar Energy — Solar Cells

1) SOLAR CELLS generate electric currents directly from sunlight. Initial costs are high but after that the energy is free and running costs almost nil.
2) Despite the cost, solar cells are the best source of energy for calculators and watches which don't use much electricity. Solar power is the only choice for remote places like Antartica and satellites.
3) Solar cells are the most expensive energy resource per Unit of electricity they produce — except for non-rechargable batteries, of course.
4) There's absolutely no pollution — and in sunny countries solar power is a very reliable source of energy — but only in the daytime.

Geothermal Energy — Heat from Underground

1) This is only possible in places where hot rocks lie quite near the surface. The source of much of the heat is the slow decay of various radioactive elements including uranium deep inside the Earth.
2) Water is pumped down to hot rocks and returns as steam to drive a generator.
3) This is actually free energy with no real environmental problems. The main drawback is the cost of drilling down several km to the hot rocks.

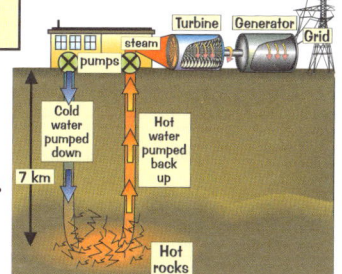

Solar Cells are like Fried Eggs — always best sunny side up...

There's a lot of details here on sources of energy — an awful lot of details. Trouble is, in the Exam they could test you on any of them, so I guess you just gotta learn 'em.

Section Five — Energy Resources & Energy Transfer

AQA Syllabus

Work Done, Energy and Power

Work, Power and Energy

When a *force* moves an *object*, ENERGY IS TRANSFERRED and WORK IS DONE

That statement sounds far more complicated than it needs to. Try this:

1) Whenever something *moves*, something else is providing some sort of "*effort*" to move it.
2) The thing putting the *effort* in needs a *supply* of energy (like *fuel* or *food* or *electricity* etc.).
3) It then does "*work*" by *moving* the object — and one way or another it *transfers* the energy it receives (as fuel) into *other forms*. 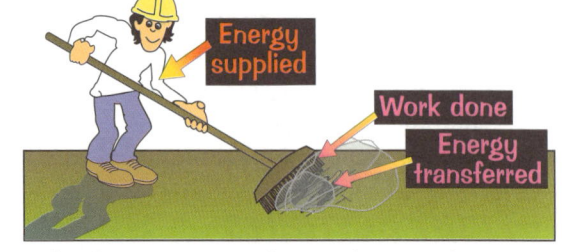
4) Whether this energy is transferred "*usefully*" (e.g. by *lifting a load*) or is "*wasted*" (e.g. lost as *friction*), you can still say that "*work is done*". Just like Batman and Bruce Wayne, "*work done*" and "*energy transferred*" are indeed "*one and the same*". (And they're both in *joules*)

It's Just Another Trivial Formula:

Work Done = Force × Distance

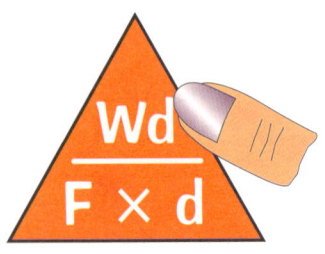

$$Wd = F \times d$$

Whether the force is *friction* or *weight* or *tension in a rope*, it's always the same. To find how much *energy* has been *transferred* (in joules), you just multiply the *force in N* by the *distance moved in m*. Easy as that. I'll show you...

EXAMPLE: Some hooligan kids drag an old tractor tyre **5m** over rough ground. They pull with a total force of **340N**. Find the energy transferred.
ANSWER: Wd = F×d = 340 × 5 = **1700J**. Phew — easy peasy isn't it?

Power is the "Rate of Doing Work" — i.e. how much per second

POWER is *not* the same thing as *force*, nor *energy*. A *powerful* machine is not necessarily one which can exert a strong *force* (though it usually ends up that way).
A POWERFUL machine is one which transfers A LOT OF ENERGY IN A SHORT SPACE OF TIME.
This is the *very easy formula* for power:

$$\text{Power} = \frac{\text{Work done}}{\text{Time taken}}$$

$$P \times t = Wd$$

EXAMPLE: A motor transfers **4.8kJ** of useful energy in **2 minutes**. Find its power output.
ANSWER: P = Wd / t = 4,800/120 = **40W** (or 40 J/s)
(Note that the kJ had to be turned into J, and the minutes into seconds.)

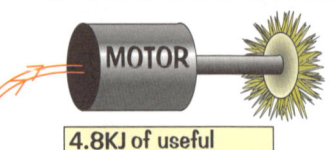

4.8KJ of useful energy in 2 minutes

Power is Measured in Watts (or J/s)

The proper unit of power is the *watt*. *One watt = 1 joule of energy transferred per second*. *Power* means 'how much energy *per second*", so *watts* are the same as "*joules per second*" (J/s). Don't ever say "watts per second" — it's *nonsense*.

Revise work done — what else...

"*Energy transferred*" and "*work done*" are the same thing. I wonder how many times I need to say that before you'll remember. Power is "*work done divided by time taken*". I wonder how many times you've got to see that before you realise you're supposed to *learn it* as well...

Kinetic and Potential Energy

Work, Power and Energy

Mass and Weight are not the same

MASS is the *amount of matter* in an object and WEIGHT is caused by the *pull* of gravity on an object. Mass is in *kg*, weight is in *newtons*. This is the *very important* formula relating *mass, weight and gravity*:

$$W = m \times g$$

(Weight = mass × g)   (See P.16)

Kinetic Energy is Energy of Movement

Anything which is *moving* has *kinetic energy*.
The *kinetic energy* of something depends both on MASS and SPEED.
The *more* it weighs and the *faster* it's going, the *bigger* its kinetic energy will be.

There's a *slightly tricky* formula for it, so you have to concentrate *a little bit harder* for this one. But hey, that's life — it can be real tough sometimes:

$$\text{Kinetic Energy} = \tfrac{1}{2} \times \text{mass} \times \text{velocity}^2$$

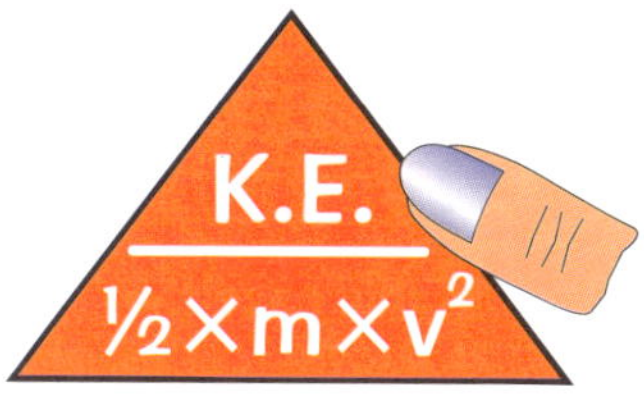

K.E. / (½ × m × v²)

EXAMPLE: A car of mass 2450kg is travelling at 38m/s. Calculate its kinetic energy.

ANSWER: It's pretty easy. You just plug the numbers into the formula but watch the "v^2"!
   KE = ½ m v² = ½ × 2450 × 38² = **1 768 900J**   (*joules* because it's *energy*)

(When the car stops suddenly, all this energy is dissipated as heat at the brakes — it's a lot of heat)

- small mass, not fast — low kinetic energy
- big fast lorries Ltd
- big mass, real fast — high kinetic energy

Elastic Potential Energy is Energy Stored in Springs

Elastic potential energy is the energy *stored* when *work is done on an object* to distort it. If a spring is either *compressed or stretched* then it is said to have *elastic potential energy*.

Gravitational Potential Energy is Energy Due to Height

Gravitational potential energy is the energy *stored in an object* because it has been raised to a specific height *against* the force of gravity.

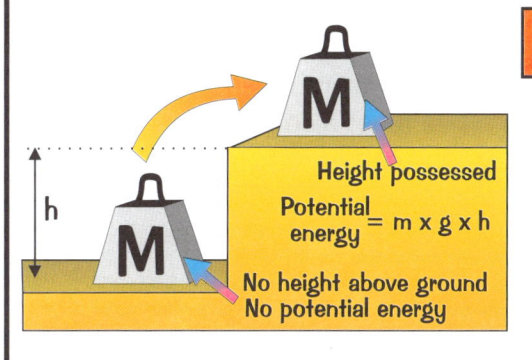

$$\text{Potential Energy} = \text{mass} \times g \times \text{height}$$

Quite often *gravitational potential energy* is just called "*potential energy*", but you should use its full name really. The proper name for g is "*gravitational field strength*". *On Earth* this has the value of $g = 10 m/s^2$ (N/kg).

P.E. / (m × g × h)

- Height possessed — Potential energy = m × g × h
- No height above ground — No potential energy

Kinetic Energy — just get a move on and learn it, OK...

Phew! A couple of tricky formulae for you here. I mean gosh they've got more than three letters in them. Still, at least they fit into formula triangles, so you may still have some small chance of getting them right. Come on, I'm joking. Formulae are always *a doddle* aren't they?

Section Five — Energy Resources & Energy Transfer   AQA Syllabus

K.E. and P.E. — Some Examples

Work, Power and Energy

1) Working out Potential Energy

EXAMPLE: A sheep of mass 47kg is slowly raised through 6.3m. Find the gain in potential energy.

ANSWER: This is pretty easy.
You just plug the numbers into the formula:
PE = mgh = 47 × 10 × 6.3 = **2 961J**
(joules because it's energy again.)

2) Calculating Your Power Output

Both cases use the same formula:

$$POWER = \frac{ENERGY\ TRANSFERRED}{TIME\ TAKEN} \quad or \quad P = \frac{E}{t}$$

a) The Timed Run Upstairs:

In this case the "energy transferred" is simply the potential energy you gain (= mgh).
Hence POWER = mgh/t

62kg, 12m, Time taken = 14s

Power output
= En. transferred/time
= mgh/t
= (62×10×12) ÷ 14
= **531W**

b) The Timed Acceleration:

This time the energy transferred is the kinetic energy you gain (= ½mv²).
Hence POWER = ½mv² /t

62kg, 0 → 8m/s, time taken = 4s

Power output
= En. transferred/time
= ½mv²/t
= (½ × 62 × 8²) ÷ 4
= **496W**

3) Calculating the Speed of Falling Objects

When something falls, its *potential energy* is *converted* into *kinetic energy*.
Hence the *further* it falls, the *faster* it goes.
In practice, some of the PE will be *dissipated* as *heat* due to *air resistance*, but in Exam questions they'll likely say you can *ignore* air resistance, in which case you'll just need to remember this *simple* and *really quite obvious* formula:

Kinetic energy GAINED = Potential Energy LOST

EXAMPLE: A mouldy tomato of mass 140g is dropped from a height of 1.7m. Calculate its speed as it hits the floor.

ANSWER: There are four key steps to this method — and you've gotta learn them:

Step 1) Find the PE lost: = mgh = 0.14 × 10 × 1.7 = **2.38J** This must also be the KE gained.

Step 2) Equate the number of Joules of KE gained to the KE formula with v in, "½mv²":
$$2.38 = ½mv²$$

Step 3) Stick the numbers in: $2.38 = ½ × 0.14 × v²$ or $2.38 = 0.07 × v²$
$2.38 ÷ 0.07 = v²$ so $v² = 34$

Step 4) Square root: $v = \sqrt{34} = $ **5.83 m/s**

Easy peasy? Not really no, but if you practise learning the four steps you'll find it's not too bad.

Revise Falling Objects — just don't lose your grip...

This is it. This is the zenith of GCSE Physics. This is the nearest it gets to *real* Physics (A-level). Look at that terrifying square root sign for a start — and a four-step method. Scary stuff.

AQA Syllabus — Section Five — Energy Resources & Energy Transfer

Magnetic Fields

Electromagnetic Forces

There's a proper definition of a <u>magnetic field</u> which you really ought to learn:

> A <u>MAGNETIC FIELD</u> is a region where <u>MAGNETIC MATERIALS</u> (like iron and steel) and also <u>WIRES CARRYING CURRENTS</u> experience <u>A FORCE</u> acting on them.

Learn all These Magnetic Field Diagrams, Arrow-perfect

They're real likely to give you one of these diagrams to do in your Exam.
So make sure you know them, especially which way the <u>arrows point</u> — <u>ALWAYS from N to S!</u>

Bar Magnet

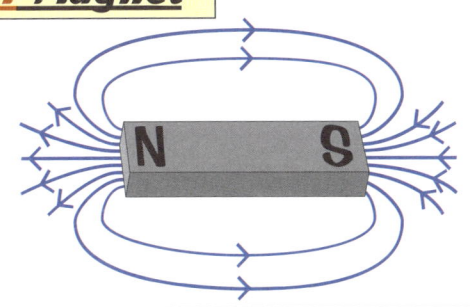

Solenoid

Same field as a bar magnet <u>outside</u>.

<u>Strong and uniform</u> field on the <u>inside</u>.

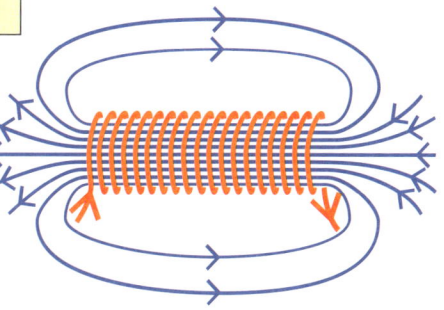

Two Bar Magnets Attracting

<u>Opposite poles ATTRACT</u>, as I'm sure you know.

Two Bar Magnets Repelling

<u>Like poles REPEL</u>, as you must surely know.

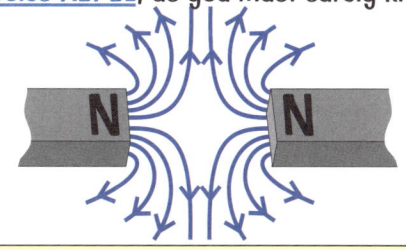

The Earth's Magnetic Field

Note that the <u>magnetic poles</u> are <u>opposite</u> to the <u>Geographic Poles</u>, i.e. the <u>south pole</u> is at the <u>North Pole</u> — if you see what I mean!

The Magnetic Field Round a Current-carrying Wire

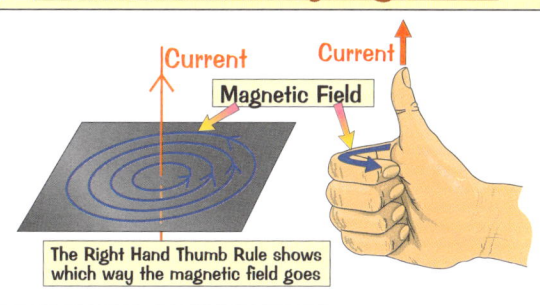

The Right Hand Thumb Rule shows which way the magnetic field goes

A Plotting Compass is a Freely Suspended Magnet

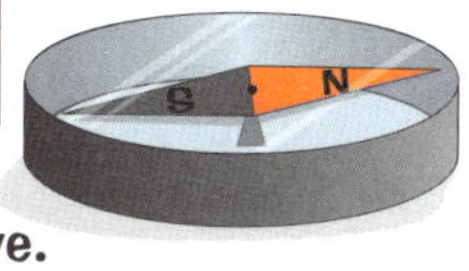

1) This means it always <u>aligns</u> itself with the <u>magnetic field</u> that it's in.
2) This is great for plotting <u>magnetic field lines</u> like around the <u>bar magnets</u> shown above.
3) Away from any magnets, it will <u>align</u> with the magnetic field of the <u>Earth</u> and point <u>North</u>.
4) <u>Any magnet</u> suspended so it can turn <u>freely</u> will also come to rest pointing <u>North-South</u>.
5) The end of the magnet which points North is called a "<u>North-seeking pole</u>" or "<u>magnetic North</u>".
   The end pointing South will therefore be a "<u>magnetic South pole</u>". This is how they got their names.

Magnetic fields — there's no getting away from them...

Mmm, this is a nice easy page for you isn't it. Learn the definition of what a magnetic field is and the six field diagrams. Also learn those five details about plotting compasses and which way the poles are compared to the Earth. Then <u>cover the page</u> and <u>scribble it all down</u>.

Section Five — Energy Resources and Energy Transfer AQA Syllabus

Electromagnets

Electromagnetic Forces

An Electromagnet is just a Coil of Wire with an Iron Core

1) *Electromagnets* are really *simple*.
2) They're simply a *solenoid* (which is just a *coil of wire*) with a piece of *"iron* inside.
3) When current *flows* through the *wires* of the solenoid it creates a *magnetic field* around it.
4) The *soft iron core* has the effect of *increasing* the *magnetic field strength*.

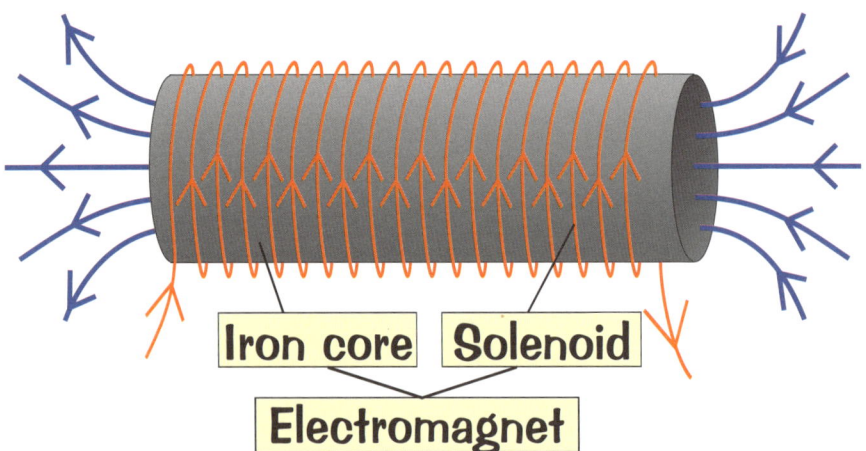

Iron core **Solenoid**
Electromagnet

1) The *magnetic field* around an *electromagnet* is just like the one round a *bar magnet*, only *stronger*.
2) This means that the *ends* of a *solenoid* act like the *North Pole* and *South Pole* of a bar magnet.
3) Pretty obviously, if the direction of the *current* is *reversed*, the N and S poles will *swap ends*.

4) If you imagine looking directly into one end of a solenoid, the *direction* of current flow tells you whether it's the *N or S pole* you're looking at, as shown by the *two diagrams* opposite. You need to remember those diagrams. They may show you a solenoid *in the Exam* and ask you which pole it is.

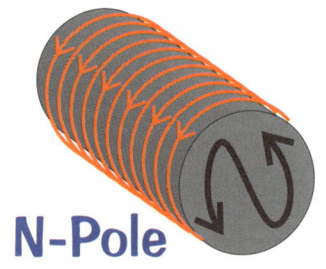

N-Pole   **S-Pole**

The STRENGTH of an ELECTROMAGNET increases if you:

1) Increase the size of the **CURRENT**.
2) Increase the number of **TURNS** the coil has.
3) Replace the **CORE** with an iron core.

Steel is Magnetically "Hard" — Ideal for Permanent Magnets

Magnetically *"hard"* means that the material *retains* its magnetism. This would be *hopeless* in an *electromagnet*, but is exactly what's required for *permanent magnets*.

N   S

Electromagnets really irritate me — I just get solenoid with them...

This is all very basic information, and really quite memorable I'd have thought. Learn the headings and diagrams first, then *cover the page* and *scribble them down*. Then gradually fill in the other details. *Keep looking back and checking*. Try to learn *all* the points. Lovely innit.

AQA Syllabus   *Section Five — Energy Resources and Energy Transfer*

The Motor Effect

Electromagnetic Forces

Anything carrying a _current_ in a _magnetic field_ will experience a _force_. There are _three important cases_:

A Current in a Magnetic Field Experiences a Force

The two tests below demonstrate the _force_ on a _current-carrying wire_ placed in a _magnetic field_. The _force_ gets _bigger_ if either the _current_ or the _magnetic field_ is made bigger.

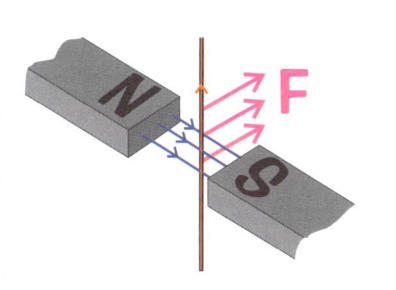

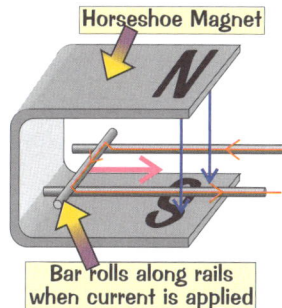

1) Note that in _both cases_ the _force_ on the wire is at _90°_ to both the _wire_ and to the _magnetic field_.
2) You can always _predict_ which way the _force_ will act using _Fleming's LHR_ as shown below.
3) To experience the _full force_, the _wire_ has to be at _90°_ to the _magnetic field_.
4) The _direction_ of the force is _reversed_ if either:
   a) the direction of the _current_ is reversed.
   b) the direction of the _magnetic field_ is reversed.

Horseshoe Magnet
Bar rolls along rails when current is applied

The Simple Electric Motor

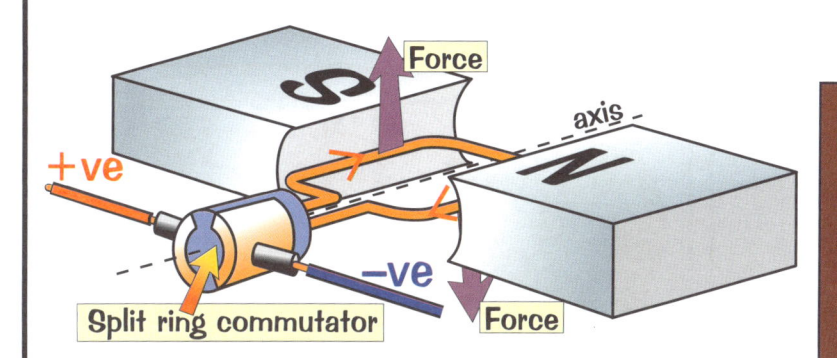

Force — axis — Force — +ve — −ve — Split ring commutator

4 Factors which Speed it up

1) More **CURRENT**
2) More **TURNS** on the coil
3) **STRONGER MAGNETIC FIELD**
4) A **IRON CORE** in the coil

1) The diagram shows the _forces_ acting on the two _side arms_ of the _coil_.
2) These forces are just the _usual forces_ which act on _any current_ in a _magnetic field_.
3) Because the coil is on a _spindle_ and the forces act _one up_ and _one down_, it _rotates_.
4) The direction of the motor can be _reversed_ either by swapping the _polarity_ of the _DC supply_ or swapping the _magnetic poles_ over.

Fleming's Left Hand Rule tells you Which way the Force Acts

1) They could test if you can do this, so _practise it_.
2) Using your _left hand_, point your _First finger_ in the direction of the _Field_ and your _seCond finger_ in the direction of the _Current_.
3) Your _thuMb_ will then point in the direction of the _force_ (_Motion_).

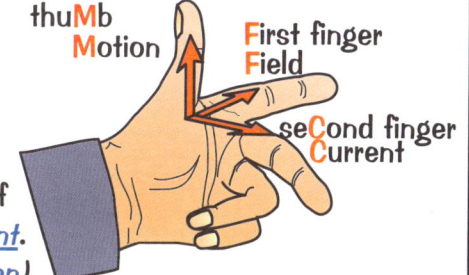

thuMb — Motion, First finger — Field, seCond finger — Current

Fleming!— how many broken wrists has he caused already...

Same old routine here. _Learn all the details_, diagrams and all, then _cover the page_ and _scribble it all down_ again _from memory_. I presume you do realise that you should be scribbling it down as scruffy as you like — because all you're trying to do is make sure that you really do _know it_.

Section Five — Energy Resources and Energy Transfer   AQA Syllabus

Electromagnetic Devices — Electromagnetic Forces

Electromagnets always have an *iron core*, which *increases the strength* of the magnet.
When the *current* is turned *off*, the magnetism *disappears* with it.
The four applications below depend on that happening.

Loudspeakers

1) *AC electrical signals* from the *amplifier* are fed to the *speaker coil* (shown red).
2) These make the coil move *back and forth* over the North pole of the *magnet*.
3) These movements make the cardboard cone *vibrate* and this creates *sounds*.

Circuit Breaker — or resettable fuse.

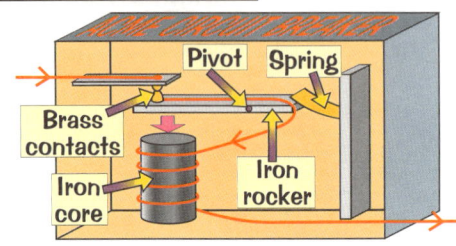

1) This is placed on the *incoming* live wire.
2) If the current gets *too high*, the *magnetic field* in the coil *pulls* the iron core which "*trips*" the switch and *breaks* the circuit.
3) It can be *reset* manually, but will always flick itself off if the *current* is *too high*.

Relay

E.g. A very big relay is used in *cars* for switching the *starter motor*, because it draws a *very big current*.

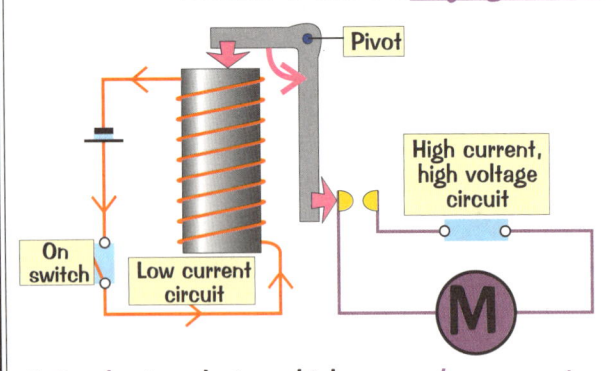

1) A *relay* is a device which uses a *low current* circuit to *switch* a *high current* circuit on/off.
2) When the switch in the low current circuit is *closed* it turns the electromagnet *ON* which *attracts* the *iron rocker*.
3) The rocker *pivots* and *closes* the contacts in the high current circuit.
4) When the low current switch is *opened*, the electromagnet *stops* pulling, the rocker returns, and the high current circuit is *broken* again.

Electric Bell

These are used in schools to stress everyone out.

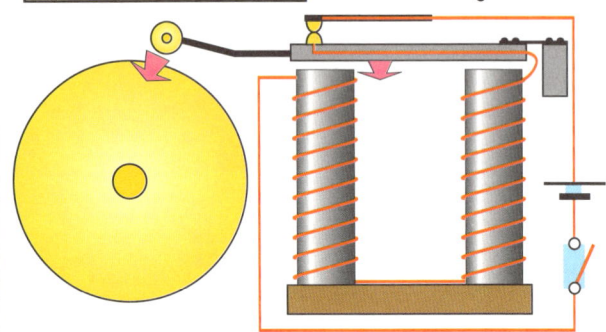

1) When the switch is *closed*, the electromagnets are turned *on*.
2) They pull the iron arm *DOWN* which *clangs* the bell, but at the same time *breaks* the contact, which immediately *turns off* the electromagnets.
3) The arm then *springs back*, which *closes* the *contact*, and off we go again...
4) The whole sequence happens *very* quickly, maybe *10 times a second*, so the bell sounds like a continuous "*brrriiiinnngg*" sound. Nice.

Only Iron, Steel and Nickel are Magnetic

Don't forget that only *iron, steel and nickel* experience a force from a magnet. So a magnet *won't stick* to *aluminium ladders* or *copper kettles* or *brass trumpets* or *gold rings* or *silver spoons*.

Learn about Magnets — it'll save you coming unstuck...

They nearly always have one of these in the Exam. Usually it's a circuit diagram of one of them and likely as not they'll ask you to explain exactly how it works. Make sure you *learn all those tricky details* for each of them. *Cover, scribble, etc...*

AQA Syllabus — Section Five — Energy Resources and Energy Transfer

Electromagnetic Induction

Sounds terrifying. Well sure it's quite mysterious, but it isn't that complicated:

ELECTROMAGNETIC INDUCTION: The creation of a _VOLTAGE_ (and maybe current) in a wire which is experiencing a _CHANGE IN MAGNETIC FIELD_.

For some reason they use the word "_induction_" rather than "_creation_", but it amounts to the _same thing_.

EM Induction — a) Field Cutting b) Field Through a Coil

Electromagnetic induction is the _induction_ of a _voltage_ and/or _current_ in a conductor.
There are _two_ different situations where you get _EM induction_. You need to know about _both_ of them:
    a) The _conductor_ moves across a _magnetic field_ and "_cuts_" through the field lines.
    b) The _magnetic field_ through a closed coil _CHANGES_, i.e. gets _bigger_ or _smaller_ or _reverses_.

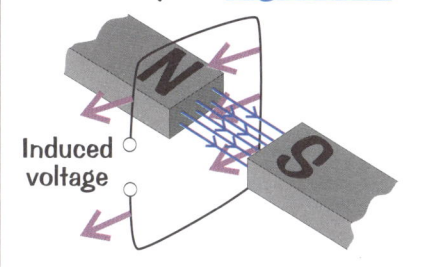

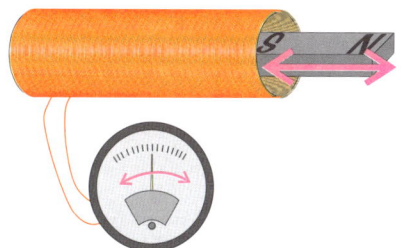

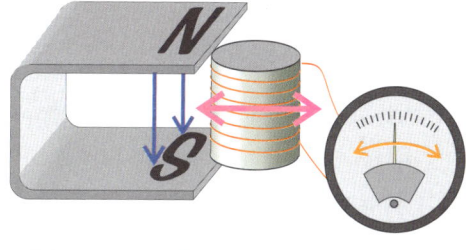

1) If the direction of _movement_ is _reversed_, then the _voltage/current_ will be _reversed_ too.
2) The current will also be reversed if the opposite pole of the magnet is shoved into the coil.

Four Factors Affect the Size of the Induced Voltage:

1) The _STRENGTH_ of the _MAGNET_   3) The _number of TURNS_ on the _COIL_
2) The _SPEED_ of movement   4) The _AREA_ of the _COIL_

Generators and Dynamos

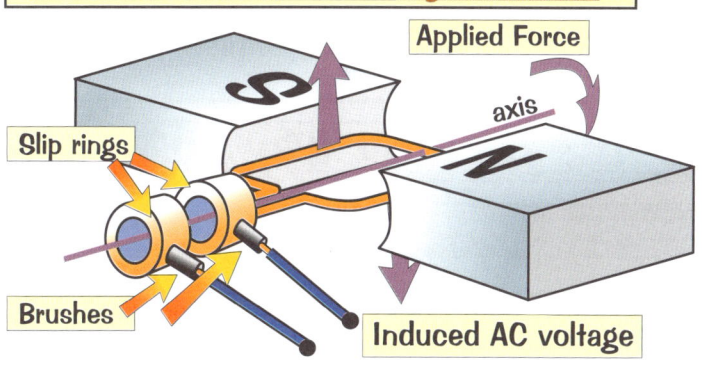

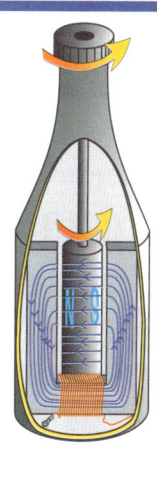

Dynamos are slightly different from _generators_ because they rotate the _magnet_. This still causes the _field through the coil_ to _swap_ every half turn, so the output is _just the same_, as shown in the CRO displays below.

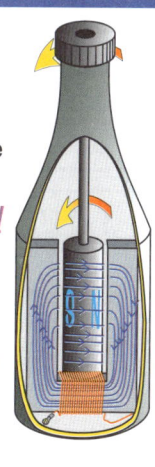

1) Generators _rotate_ a coil in a _magnetic field_.
2) Their _construction_ is pretty much like a _motor_.
3) The _difference_ is the _slip rings_ which are in _constant contact_ with the brushes, so the contacts _don't swap_ every ½ turn.
4) This means they produce _AC voltage_, as shown by the _CRO displays_. Note that _faster_ revs produce not only _more_ peaks but _higher_ overall voltage too.

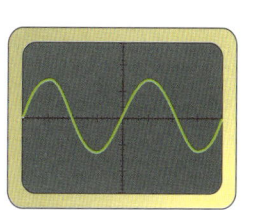

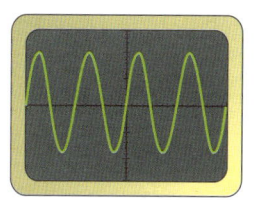

"Electromagnetic Induction" — pretty tricky stuff...

"Electromagnetic Induction" gets my vote for "Definitely Most Trickiest Topic To Learn". If it wasn't so important maybe you wouldn't have to bother learning it. The trouble is this is how all our electricity is generated. So it's pretty important. _Learn and scribble_ ...

Section Five — Energy Resources and Energy Transfer   AQA Syllabus

Transformers — Electromagnetic Induction

Transformers use *Electromagnetic Induction*.   So they will *only* work on *AC*.

Transformers Change the Voltage — but only AC Voltages

1) *Step-up* transformers step the voltage *up*. They have *more turns* on the secondary coil.
2) *Step-down* transformers step the voltage *down*. They have *fewer turns* on the secondary. They drop the voltage from 400,000V to a "safe" 230V for our homes.

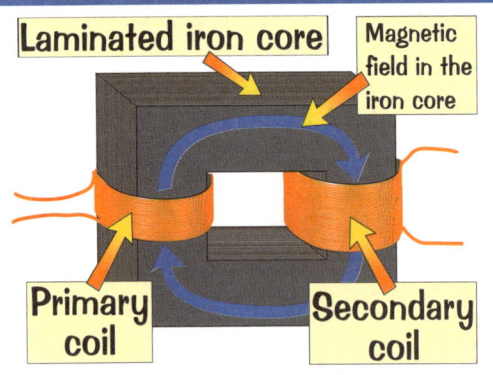

1) The *laminated iron core* is purely for transferring the *magnetic field* from the primary coil to the secondary.
2) The iron core is *laminated* with layers of *insulation* to reduce the *eddy currents* which *heat it up*, and therefore *waste energy*.

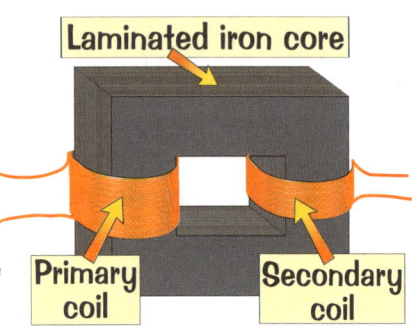

1) The primary coil produces *a magnetic field* which stays within the *iron core* and this means it *all* passes through the *secondary* coil.
2) Because there is *alternating current* (AC) in the *primary* coil, this means that the magnetic field in the iron core is *reversing* (50 times a second, usually) — i.e. it's a *changing* field.
3) This rapidly *changing* magnetic field is then experienced by the *secondary coil* and this *induces* an *alternating voltage* in it — *electromagnetic induction* of a voltage in fact.
4) The *relative number of turns* on the two coils determines whether the voltage created in the secondary is *greater* or *less* than the voltage in the primary.
5) If you supplied DC to the primary, you'd get *NOTHING* out of the secondary at all. Sure, there'd still be a field in the iron core, but it wouldn't be *constantly changing* so there'd be no *induction* in the secondary because you need a *changing field* to induce a voltage. Don't you! So don't forget it — transformers only work with *AC*. They won't work with DC *at all*.

The Transformer Equation — use it Either Way Up

In words: The *RATIO OF TURNS* on the two coils equals the *RATIO OF THEIR VOLTAGES*.

$$\frac{\text{Primary Voltage}}{\text{Secondary Voltage}} = \frac{\text{Number of turns on Primary}}{\text{Number of turns on Secondary}}$$

$$\frac{V_P}{V_S} = \frac{N_P}{N_S} \quad \text{or} \quad \frac{V_S}{V_P} = \frac{N_S}{N_P}$$

Well, it's *just another formula*. You stick in the numbers *you've got* and work out the one *that's left*. It's real useful to remember you can write it *either way up* — this example's much trickier algebra-wise if you start with V_S on the bottom...

EXAMPLE: A transformer has 40 turns on the primary and 800 on the secondary. If the input voltage is 1000V find the output voltage.

ANSWER: $V_S/V_P = N_S/N_P$ so $V_S/1000 = 800/40$ $V_S = 1000 \times (800/40) = \underline{20{,}000V}$

The ubiquitous Iron Core — where would we be without it...

Besides their iron core transformers have lots of other *important* details which also need to be *learnt*. You'll need to practise with that tricky equations too. It's unusual because it can't be put into formula triangles, but other than that the method is the same. Just *practise*.

AQA Syllabus — Section Five — ENERGY RESOURCES AND ENERGY TRANSFER

The National Grid

Electromagnetic Induction

1) The _National Grid_ is the _network_ of pylons and cables which _covers_ the whole country.
2) It takes electricity from the _power stations_, to just where it's needed in _homes_ and _industry_.
3) It enables power to be _generated_ anywhere on the grid, and to then be _supplied_ anywhere else on the grid.

All Power Stations are Pretty Much the Same

They all have a _boiler_ of some sort, which makes _steam_ which drives a _turbine_ which drives a _generator_. The generator produces _electricity_ (by _induction_) by _rotating_ an _electromagnet_ within coils of wire (see P. 78).

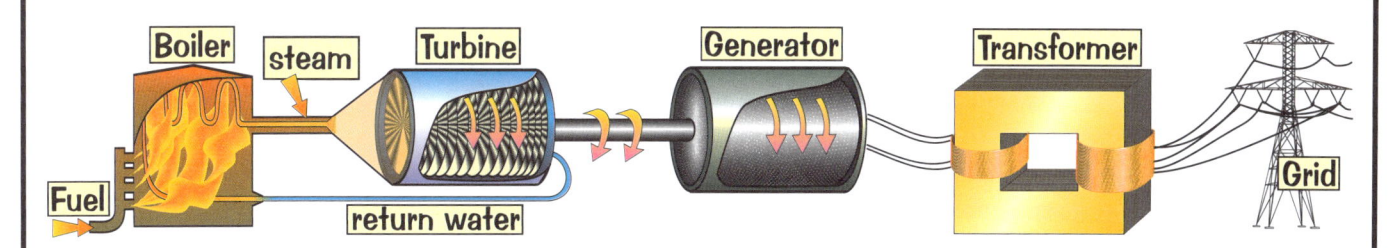

Learn all these features of the _NATIONAL GRID_ — power stations, transformers, pylons, etc:

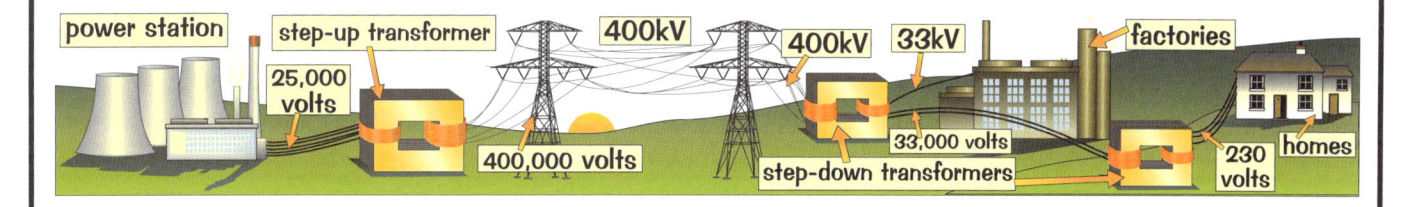

Pylon Cables are at 400,000 V to keep the Current Low

You need to understand why the _VOLTAGE_ is so _HIGH_ and why it's _AC_. Learn these points.

1) The formula for _power supplied_ is: _Power = Voltage × Current_ or: _P = V×I_
2) So to transmit a _lot_ of power, you either need high _voltage_ or high _current_.
3) The problem with _high current_ is the _loss_ (as heat) due to the _resistance_ of the cables.
4) It's much _cheaper_ to boost the voltage up to _400,000V_ and keep the current _very low_.
5) This requires _transformers_ as well as _big_ pylons with _huge_ insulators, but it's still _cheaper_.
6) The transformers have to _step_ the voltage _up_ at one end, for _efficient_ transmission, and then bring it back down to _safe_ useable levels at the other end.

400,000 volts? — that could give you a bit of a buzz...

Quite a few tricky details on this page. The power station and National Grid are easy enough, but fully explaining why pylon cables are at 400,000V is a bit trickier — but you do need to learn it. When you watch TV think of the rout the electricity has to travel. _Scribble it down_.

Section Five — Energy Resources and Energy Transfer *AQA Syllabus*

Revision Summary for Section Five

There are three distinct parts to Section Five. First there's power, work done, efficiency etc. which involves a lot of formulae and calculations. Then there's heat transfer, which is trickier to fully get the grip of than most people realise, and finally there's the stuff on generating power, which is basically easy but there are lots of drivelly details to learn. Make sure you realise the different approach needed for all three bits and focus your planet-sized brain accordingly.

1) List the ten different types of energy, and give twelve examples of energy transfers.
2) What causes heat to flow from one place to another? What do molecules do as they heat up?
3) Give a strict definition of conduction of heat and say which materials are good conductors.
4) Why are metals such good conductors?
5) Give a strict definition of convection. Give two examples of natural and forced convection.
6) List five properties of heat radiation. Which surfaces emit heat radiation best?
7) Describe two experiments to demonstrate the effect of different surfaces on radiant heat.
8) Describe insulation measures which reduce a) conduction   b) convection   c) radiation.
9) List the seven main ways of insulating houses. Say which are the most *effective* and which are the most *cost-effective* measures. How do you decide on cost-effectiveness?
10) Which types of heat transfer are insulated against in: a) double glazing; b) draught proofing.
11) Sketch the basic energy flow diagram for a typical "useful device".
12) What forms does the wasted energy always take?
13) What's the formula for efficiency? What are the three numerical forms suitable for efficiency?
14) List the four non-renewable sources of energy and eight sources of renewable energy.
15) Which kind of resources do we get most of our energy from?
16) List the broad advantages and disadvantages of using renewable or non-renewable sources of energy. What does it mean when a question says "Discuss..."?
17) List seven environmental hazards with non-renewables and four ways that we can use less.
18) Give full details of how we can use wind power, including the advantages and disadvantages.
19) Give full details of how a hydroelectric scheme works.
20) Explain the principles of wood-burning for generating electricity. Give the pros and cons.
21) Sketch a wave generator and explain the pros and cons of this as a source of energy.
22) Explain how tidal power can be harnessed. What are the pros and cons of this idea?
23) Give brief details, with a diagram, of solar power.
24) Explain where geothermal energy comes from. Describe how we can make use of it.
25) What's the connection between "work done" and "energy transferred"?
26) What's the formula for work done? A crazy dog drags a big branch 12m over the next-door neighbour's front lawn, pulling with a force of 535N. How much energy was transferred?
27) What's the formula for power? What are the units of power?
28) Write down the formulae for KE and PE. Find the KE of a 78kg sheep moving at 23m/s.
29) Calculate the power output of a 78kg sheep which runs up a 20m staircase in 16.5 seconds.
30) Calculate the speed of a 78kg sheep as it hits the floor from a height of 20m.
31) If the sheep bounces back up to a height of 18m calculate the % loss of KE at the bounce.
32) Draw magnetic field diagrams for a) solenoid, b) 2 bar magnets repelling, c) Earth's magnetic field.
33) What is an electromagnet made of? How can you tell the polarity of the ends?
34) What is meant by magnetically hard?
35) Sketch and give details of: a) Loudspeaker, b) Circuit breaker, c) Relay, d) Electric bell.
36) Give the definition of electromagnetic induction. Sketch three examples.
37) List the four factors which affect the size of the induced voltage.
38) Sketch a generator with all the details.
39) Sketch the two types of transformer, and highlight the main details. Explain how they work.
40) Sketch a typical power station, and the National Grid and explain why it's at 400kV.

AQA Syllabus

Section Five — Energy Resources and Energy Transfer

Radioactivity

Types of Radiation

Types, Properties & Uses of Radioactivity

Don't get *mixed up* between *nuclear* radiation which is *dangerous* — and *electromagnetic* radiation which *generally isn't*. Gamma radiation is included in both, of course.
A substance which gives out radiation all the time is called *radioactive*.

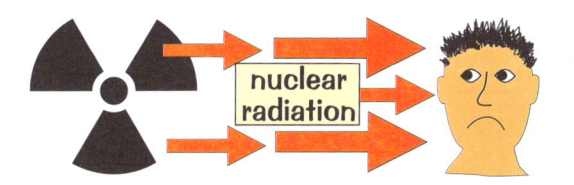

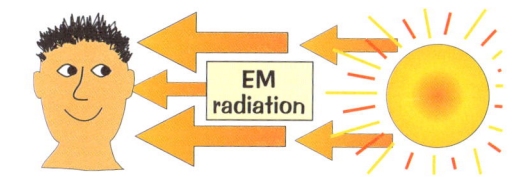

Nuclear Radiation: Alpha, Beta and Gamma (α, β and γ)

You need to remember *three things* about *each type of radiation*:
1) What they actually *are*.
2) How well they *penetrate* materials.
3) How strongly they *ionise* that material (i.e. bash into atoms and *knock electrons off*).
   There's a pattern: The *further* the radiation can *penetrate* before hitting an atom and getting stopped, the *less damage* it will do along the way and so the *less ionising* it is.

Alpha Particles are Helium Nuclei

1) They are relatively *big* and *heavy* and *slow moving*.
2) They therefore *don't* penetrate into materials but are *stopped quickly*.
3) Because of their size they are *strongly* ionising, which just means they *bash into* a lot of atoms and *knock electrons off* them before they slow down, which creates lots of ions — hence the term *"ionising"*.

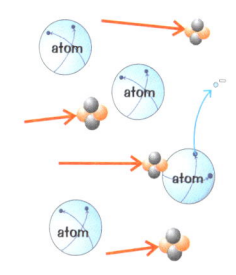

Beta Particles are Electrons

1) These are *in between* alpha and gamma in terms of their *properties*.
2) They move *quite* fast and they are *quite* small (they're electrons).
3) They *penetrate moderately* before colliding and are *moderately ionising* too.
4) For every *β–particle* emitted, a *neutron* turns to a *proton* in the nucleus.

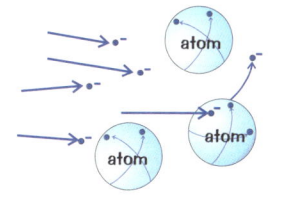

Gamma Rays are Very Short Wavelength EM Waves

1) They are the *opposite* of alpha particles in a way.
2) They *penetrate a long way* into materials without being stopped.
3) This means they are *weakly* ionising because they tend to *pass through* rather than colliding with atoms. Eventually they *hit something* and do *damage*.

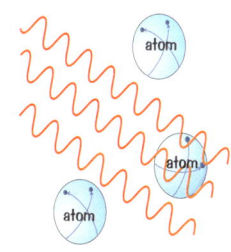

Learn the three types of radiation — it's easy as abc...

Alpha, beta and gamma. You do realise those are just the first three letters of the Greek alphabet don't you: α, β, γ — just like a, b, c. They might sound like complex names to you but they were just easy labels at the time. Anyway, *learn all the facts* about them — and *scribble*.

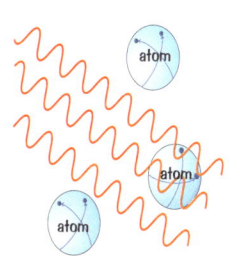

Section Six — Radioactivity AQA Syllabus

Background Radiation

Types, Properties & Uses of Radioactivity

Remember What Blocks the Three Types of Radiation...

As radiation _passes through_ materials some of the radiation is _absorbed_. The greater the _thickness_ of material the _more absorption_.

They really like this for Exam questions, so make sure _you know_ what it takes to _block_ each of the _three_:

ALPHA particles are blocked by _paper_.
BETA particles are blocked by thin _aluminium_.
GAMMA rays are blocked by _thick lead_.

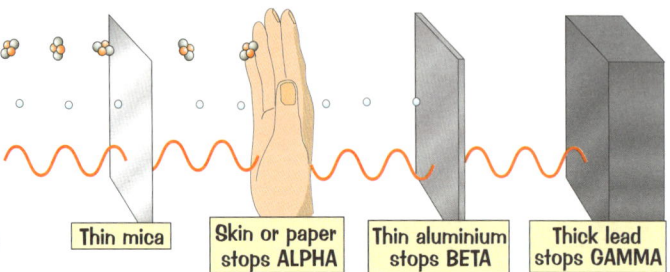

Thin mica | Skin or paper stops ALPHA | Thin aluminium stops BETA | Thick lead stops GAMMA

Of course anything _equivalent_ will also block them, e.g. _skin_ will stop _alpha_, but _not_ the others; a thin sheet of _any metal_ will stop _beta_; and _very thick concrete_ will stop _gamma_ just like lead does.

Background Radiation Comes From Many Sources

Natural background radiation comes from:

1) Radioactivity of naturally occurring _unstable isotopes_ which are _all around us_ — in the _air_, in _food_, in _building materials_ and in the _rocks_ under our feet.

2) Radiation from _space_, which is known as _cosmic rays_. These come mostly from the _Sun_.

3) Radiation due to _human activity_. i.e. _fallout_ from _nuclear explosions_ or _dumped nuclear waste_. But this represents a _tiny_ proportion of the total background radiation.

The **RELATIVE PROPORTIONS** of _background radiation_:

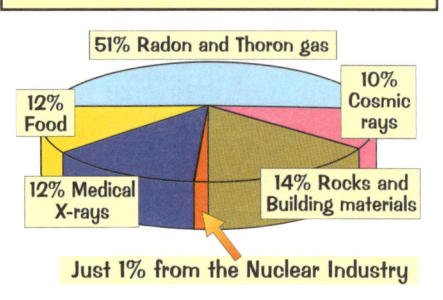

- 51% Radon and Thoron gas
- 10% Cosmic rays
- 12% Food
- 12% Medical X-rays
- 14% Rocks and Building materials
- Just 1% from the Nuclear Industry

The Level of Background Radiation Changes, Depending on Where You Are

1) At _high altitudes_ (e.g. in _jet planes_) it _increases_ because of more exposure to _cosmic rays_.

2) _Underground in mines_, etc. it increases because of the _rocks_ all around. Rocks like _granite_ have a high background count rate.

3) Certain _underground rocks_ can cause higher levels at the _surface_, especially if they release _radioactive radon gas_, which tends to get trapped _inside people's houses_. This varies widely across the UK depending on the _rock type_, as shown:

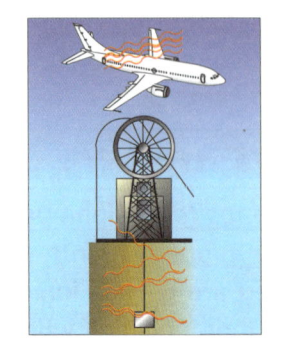

Coloured bits indicate more radiation from rocks

Background Radiation — it's no good burying your head in the sand...

Yip, it's funny old stuff is radiation, that's for sure. It is quite mysterious, I guess, but just like anything else, the _more you learn about it_, the _less_ of a mystery it becomes. This page is positively bristling with simple straightforward facts about radiation. Three tiny little _mini-essays_ practised two or three times and all this knowledge will be yours — forever. Enjoy. ☺

AQA Syllabus

Section Six — Radioactivity

Radiation Hazards and Safety

Types, Properties & Uses of Radioactivity

Radiation Harms Living Cells

1) *Alpha*, *beta* and *gamma* radiation will cheerfully enter living cells and *collide* with molecules.
2) These collisions cause *ionisation*, which *damages* or *destroys* the molecules.
3) *Lower* doses tend to cause *minor* damage without *killing* the cell.
4) This can give rise to *mutant* cells which divide *uncontrollably*. This is *cancer*.
5) *Higher* doses tend to *kill cells* completely, which causes *radiation sickness* if a lot of your body cells *all get blatted at once*.
6) The *extent* of the harmful effects depends on *two things*:
    a) How much *exposure* you have to the radiation.
    b) The *energy* and *penetration* of the radiation emitted, since some types are *more hazardous* than others, of course.

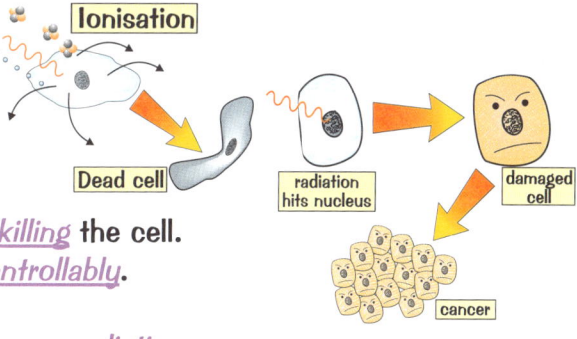

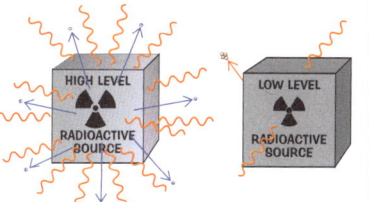

Outside The Body, β and γ Sources are the Most Dangerous

This is because *beta and gamma* can get *inside* to the delicate *organs*, whereas alpha is much less dangerous because it *can't penetrate* the skin.

Inside The Body, an α Source is the Most Dangerous

Inside the body alpha-sources do all their damage in a *very localised area*. Beta and gamma sources on the other hand are *less dangerous* inside the body because they mostly *pass straight out* without doing much damage.

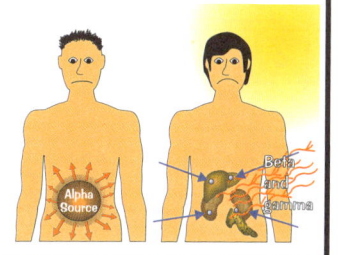

You Need to Learn These Safety Precautions

I'm sure you already know that radioactive materials need to be handled *carefully*. In the Exam they might ask you to list some *specific precautions* that should be taken when handling *radioactive materials*. If you want those *easy marks* you'd better learn all these:

In the School Laboratory:

1) *Never* allow *skin contact* with a source. Always handle with *tongs*.
2) Keep the source at *arm's length* to keep it *as far* from the body *as possible*.
3) Keep the source *pointing away* from the body and avoid looking *directly at it*.
4) *Always* keep the source in a *lead box* and put it back in *as soon* as the experiment is *over*.

Radiation can also treat cancer as well as cause it:

Radiotherapy — the Treatment of Cancer Using γ Rays

Since high doses of gamma rays will *kill all living cells* they can be used to *treat cancers*. The gamma rays have to be directed *carefully* and at just the right *dosage* so as to kill the *cancer cells* without damaging too many *normal cells*.

Radiation Sickness — well yes, it does all get a bit tedious...

Quite a few picky details here. It's easy to kid yourself that you don't really need to know all this stuff. Well take it from me, you *do* need to know it all and there's only one surefire way to find out whether you do or not. Three *mini-essays* please, with all the picky details in. Enjoy.

Uses of Radioactive Materials

Types, Properties & Uses of Radioactivity

This is a nice _easy bit_ of straightforward learning. Below are _three uses_ for radioactive isotopes. Make sure you _learn all_ the details. In particular, make sure you get the grip of why each application uses a _particular radio-isotope_ according to its _half-life_ and the _type of radiation_ it gives out.

1) Tracers in Medicine — always Short Half-life γ emitters

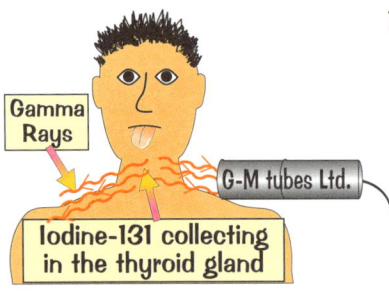

1) Certain _radioactive isotopes_ can be _injected_ into people (or they can just _swallow_ them) and their progress _around the body_ can be followed using a _detector_, with a computer to convert the reading to a _TV display_ showing where the _strongest_ reading is coming from. A well known example is the use of _Iodine-131_ which is absorbed by the _thyroid gland_, just like normal Iodine-127, but it gives out _radiation_ which can be _detected_ to indicate whether or not the thyroid gland is _taking in the iodine_ as it should.

2) _Isotopes_ which are taken _into the body_ should be _GAMMA sources_ so that the radiation _passes out_ of the body. They must also have a _short_ half-life, preferably of just _a few hours_, so that the radioactivity inside the patient _quickly_ disappears.

2) Tracers in Industry — For Finding Leaks

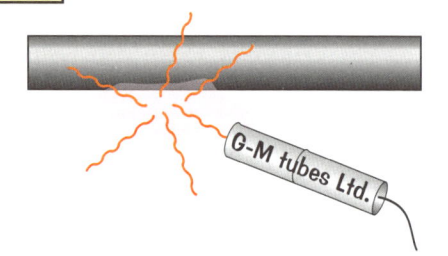

This is _much the same technique_ as the medical tracers.
1) Radio-isotopes can be used to detect _leaks_ in pipes.
2) You just _squirt it in_, and then go along the _outside_ of the pipe with a _detector_ to find areas of _extra high_ radioactivity, which indicates the stuff is _leaking out_. This is really useful for _concealed_ or _underground_ pipes, to save you digging up half the road trying to find the leak.
3) The isotope used _must_ be a _gamma emitter_, so that the radiation can be _detected_ even through _metal or earth_ which may be _surrounding_ the pipe. Alpha and beta rays wouldn't be much use because they are easily _blocked_ by any surrounding material.
4) It should also have a _short half-life_ so as not to cause a _hazard_ if it collects somewhere.

3) Radioactive Dating of Rocks and Archaeological Specimens

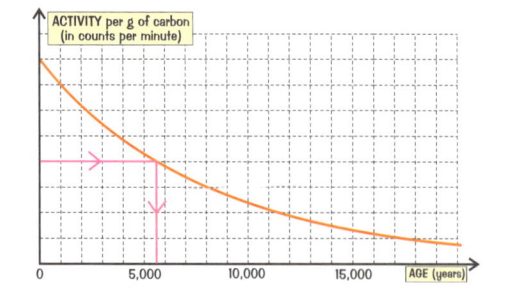

1) The discovery of radioactivity and the idea of _half-life_ gave scientists their _first opportunity_ to _accurately_ work out the _age_ of _rocks_ and _fossils_ and archaeological specimens.
2) By measuring the _amount_ of a _radioactive isotope_ left in a sample, and knowing its _half-life_, you can work out _how long_ the thing has been around.
3) The half-life of a radioactive substance is the _time taken_ for the number of _parent atoms_ in a sample to _halve_.
4) It can also be defined as the _time taken_ for the count rate from the original source to fall to _half its initial level_. (See P. 87)

Will any of that be in your Exam? — isotope so...

First _learn_ the three headings till you can write them down _from memory_. Then start _learning_ all the details that go with each one of them. As usual, the best way to check what you know is to do a _mini-essay_ for each section. Then check back and see what details you _missed_. Nicely.

Atomic Structure

Atomic Structure & Nuclear Fission

You can look at the Chemistry Book for a few more details on the structure of atoms.

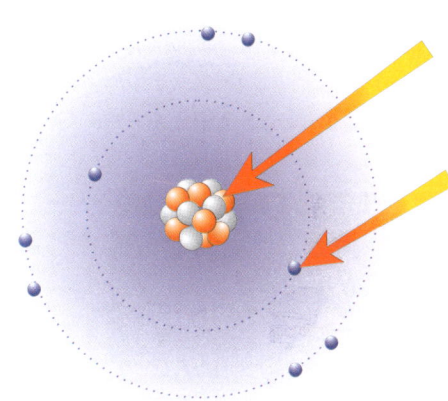

The **NUCLEUS** contains *protons* and *neutrons*.
Most of the **MASS** of the atom is contained in the *nucleus*, but it takes up virtually *no space* — it's *tiny*.

The **ELECTRONS** fly around the *outside*.
They're *negatively charged* and really really *small*.
They occupy *a lot of space* and this gives the atom its *overall size*, even though it's mostly *empty space*.
The number of electrons is *equal to* the number of protons.
This means that the whole atom has *no overall charge*.

Make sure you *learn this table*:

PARTICLE	MASS	CHARGE
Proton	1	+1
Neutron	1	0
Electron	1/2000	−1

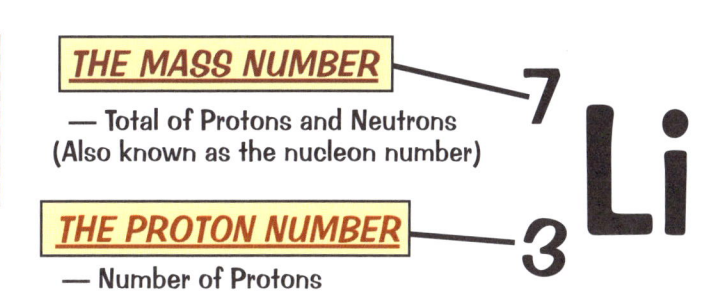

THE MASS NUMBER
— Total of Protons and Neutrons
(Also known as the nucleon number)

THE PROTON NUMBER
— Number of Protons

$$^{7}_{3}\text{Li}$$

Rutherford's Scattering and the Demise of the Plum Pudding

1) In 1804 *John Dalton* said matter was made up of tiny *solid spheres* which he called *atoms*.

2) Later they discovered *electrons* could be *removed* from atoms. They then saw atoms as *spheres* of *positive charge* with tiny negative electrons *stuck in them* like plums in a *plum pudding*.

3) Then *Ernest Rutherford* and his merry men tried firing *alpha particles* at *thin gold foil*. Most of them just went *straight through*, but the odd one came straight *back at them*, which was frankly a bit of a *shocker* for Ernie and his pals. Being pretty clued up guys though they realised this meant that *most* of the mass of the atom was concentrated *at the centre* in a *tiny nucleus*, with a *positive charge*.
This means that most of an atom is just made up of *empty space*, which is also *a bit of a shocker* when you think about it.

Plum Pudding Theory — by 1911 they'd had their fill of it...

Yeah, that's right — *atoms* are mostly *empty space*. When you think about it, those electrons are amazing little jokers really. They have almost no mass, no size, and a tiny little −ve charge. In the end it's only their frantic whizzing about that makes atoms what they are. It's outrageous.

Section Six — Radioactivity

AQA Syllabus

Nuclear Fission

Atomic Structure & Nuclear Fission

Nuclear Fission — The Splitting Up of Uranium Atoms

Nuclear power stations and nuclear submarines are both powered by nuclear reactors. In a nuclear reactor, a controlled chain reaction takes place in which uranium atoms split up and release energy in the form of heat. This heat is then simply used to heat water to drive a steam turbine. So nuclear reactors are really just glorified steam engines!

The Chain Reaction:

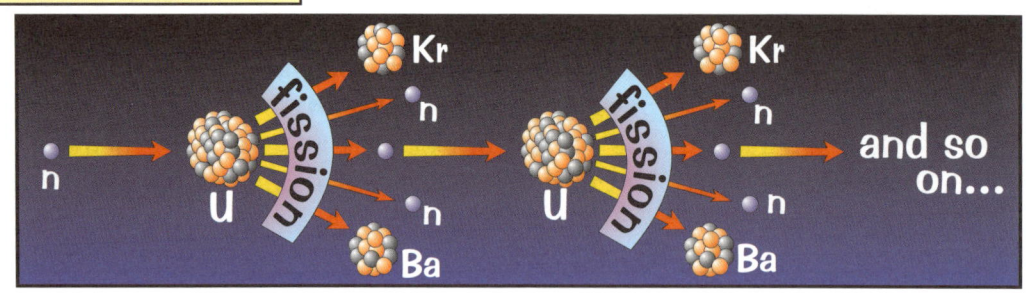

1) Each time a uranium atom splits up, it spits out two or three neutrons, one of which hits another uranium nucleus, causing it to split also, and thus keeping the chain reaction going.
2) When a uranium atom splits in two it will form two new lighter elements. These new nuclei are usually radioactive because they have the "wrong" number of neutrons in them.
   This is the big problem with nuclear power — it produces huge amounts of radioactive material which is very difficult and expensive to dispose of safely.
3) Each nucleus splitting (called a fission) gives out a lot of energy — a lot more energy than you get with a chemical bond between two atoms. Make sure you remember that. Nuclear processes release much more energy than chemical processes do. That's why nuclear bombs are so much more powerful than ordinary bombs (which rely on chemical reactions).

Decay Processes of α, β and γ Emission

1) Alpha Emission:

A typical alpha-emission: $^{226}_{88}Ra \rightarrow ^{222}_{86}Rn + ^{4}_{2}He$ (Alpha particle)

An α-particle is simply a helium nucleus, mass 4 and charge of +2 made up of 2 protons and 2 neutrons.

2) Beta Emission:

A typical beta-emission: $^{14}_{6}C \rightarrow ^{14}_{7}N + ^{0}_{-1}e$ (Beta particle)

A β-particle is simply an electron, with no mass and a charge of -1. Every time a beta particle is emitted from the nucleus, a neutron in the nucleus is converted to a proton.

3) Gamma Emission:

A typical combined α and γ emission: $^{238}_{92}U \rightarrow ^{234}_{90}Th + ^{4}_{2}He + ^{0}_{0}\gamma$ (Gamma ray)

A γ-ray is a photon with no mass and no charge.
After an alpha or beta emission the nucleus sometimes has extra energy to get rid of. It does this by emitting a gamma ray. Gamma emission never changes the proton or mass numbers of the nucleus.

Alpha give the odd mistake — just don't beta lazy to learn it...

Learn all the details about chain reactions in nuclear fission with one easy mini-essay. Also, more details about those three lovely types of radiation: alpha particles, beta particles and gamma rays. That's it so cover the page and jot down all the juicy details.

AQA Syllabus — *Section Six — Radioactivity*

Half-life

Atomic Structure & Nuclear Fission

The Radioactivity of a Sample Always Decreases Over Time

1) This is *pretty obvious* when you think about it. Each time a *decay* happens and an alpha, beta or gamma is given out, it means one more *radioactive* nucleus has *disappeared*.

2) Obviously, as the *unstable nuclei* all steadily disappear, the *activity* as a whole will also *decrease*. So the *older* a sample becomes, the *less* radiation it will emit.

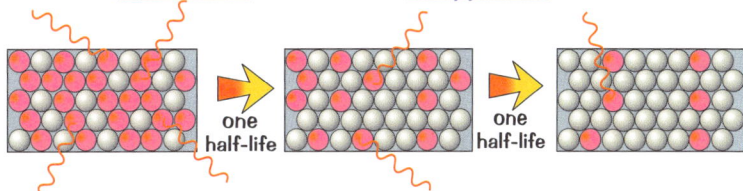

3) *How quickly* the activity *drops off* varies a lot from one radio-isotope to another. For *some* it can take *just a few hours* before nearly all the unstable nuclei have *decayed*, whilst others can last for *millions of years*.

4) The problem with trying to *measure* this is that the activity *never reaches ZERO*, which is why we have to use the idea of *HALF-LIFE* to measure how quickly the activity *drops off*.

5) Learn this *important definition* of *half-life*:

> **HALF-LIFE is the TIME TAKEN for THE NUMBER OF PARENT atoms in a sample to HALVE**

(The number of parent atoms is the number of atoms in the original radioactive source)

Another definition of half-life is: "*The time taken for the activity (or count rate) of the original substance to fall to half it's original level*". Use either.

6) A *short half-life* means the activity falls *quickly*, because *lots* of the nuclei decay *quickly*.

7) A *long half-life* means the activity falls *more slowly* because *most* of the nuclei don't decay for a *long time* — they just sit there, basically *unstable*, but kind of *biding their time*.

Measuring the Half-life of a Sample Using a graph

1) *Several readings* are taken of *count rate* and the results can then be *plotted* as a *graph*, which will *always* be shaped like the one below.

2) The *half-life* is found from the graph, by finding the *time interval* on the *bottom axis* corresponding to a *halving* of the *activity* on the *vertical axis*. Easy peasy really.

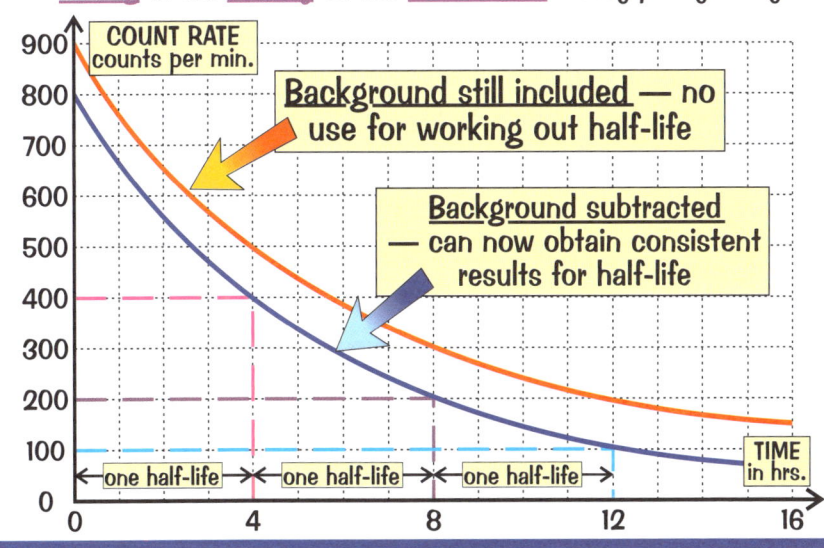

One trick you really do need to know about is the business of the *background radiation*, which also adds to the count and gives *false readings*. You have to measure the background count *first* and then *subtract it* from *every* reading you get, before plotting the results on the *graph*. Realistically, the only *difficult bit* is actually *remembering* about that for your *Exam*, should they ask you about it.

Definition of Half-life — a freshly woken teenager...

People can get really confused by the idea of half-life. Remember — a radioactive sample will *never* completely decay away because the amount left just keeps *halving*. So the only way to measure how long it "lasts", is to time how long it takes to drop by half. That's all it is. *Peasy*.

Revision Summary for Section Six

It's an outrage — just so much stuff you've gotta learn — it's all work, work, work, no time to rest, no time to play. But then that's the grim cruel reality of life in 1990's Britain — just drudgery, hard work and untold weariness...   "And then he woke up and it had all been a dream..."   Yeah, maybe life's not so bad after all — even for hard-done-by teenagers. Just a few jolly bits and bobs to learn in warm, cosy, comfortable civilisation. Practise these questions over and over again till you can answer them all effortlessly. Smile and enjoy. ☺

1) What is the main difference between EM radiation and nuclear radiation?
2) Describe in detail the nature and properties of the three types of radiation: α, β, and γ.
3) How do the three types compare in penetrating power and ionising power?
4) List several things which will block each of the three types.
5) Sketch a fairly accurate pie chart to show the six main sources of background radiation.
6) List three places where the level of background radiation is increased and explain why.
7) Exactly what kind of damage does radiation do inside body cells?
8) What damage does low doses cause? What effects do higher doses have?
9) Which kind of sources are most dangerous a) inside the body   b) outside the body?
10) List four safety precautions for when handling radioactive materials.
11) Describe a situation where the killing of living cells by gamma rays can be helpful.
12) Describe in detail how radioactive isotopes are used in each of the following:
    a) tracers in medicine   b) tracers in industry   c) dating of rock samples
13) Sketch an atom. Give three details about the nucleus and the electrons.
14) Draw up a wee table detailing the mass and charge of the three basic subatomic particles.
15) Explain what the mass number and proton number of an atom represent.
16) Write down the number of electrons, protons and neutrons there are in an atom of $^{226}_{88}Ra$, and say what its overall charge would be.
17) What was the Plum Pudding Model? Who put paid to that crazy old idea?
18) Describe Rutherford's Scattering Experiment with a diagram and say what happened.
19) What was the inevitable conclusion to be drawn from this experiment?
20) Draw a diagram to illustrate the fission of uranium and explain how the chain reaction works.
21) Describe the decay processes of: a) alpha particles b) beta particles c) gamma rays.
22) Sketch a diagram to show how the activity of a sample keeps halving.
23) Give a proper definition of half-life. How long and how short can half-lives be?
24) Sketch a typical graph of activity against time. Show how the half-life can be found.

Answers

P.25 Revn Sumy: 5) 0.09m/s, 137m   7) 35m/s^2 15) 7.5m/s^2 16) 5.7kg
P.32: 1) 330m/s   2) 200kHz
P.40: 1) 198m   2) 490m
P.45 Revn Sumy: 20) a) 500,000 Hz   b) 0.35m   c) 4,600,000 Hz   d) 0.04m/s   e) 150s   21) 150m/s   22) 2×10^{11}Hz
P.56 Revn Sumy: 38) Real strange, The Bentley Turbo
P.80 Revn Sumy: 26) 6420J   28) 20,631J   29) 945W   30) 20m/s   31) 10%

Index

A
absorbed 33, 34
absorbing 61
AC 76, 77, 78, 79
acceleration
 16, 17, 18, 19, 20, 21, 22
acetate rod 12
Africa 42
air resistance 21, 22
alpha particles/emission
 81, 82, 83, 84, 86, 87
alternating current
 See AC
ammeters 1, 3, 7
amplitude 26, 37
amps 1
analogue signals 36
Andes 43
angles of incidence, reflection and refraction 27, 28
annual saving 63
aquaplaning 24
arctic circle 46
argon 40
artificial satellites 49
Atlantic 44
atomic structure 85
attraction
 12, 51, 55, 73

B
background radiation
 82, 87
balanced forces 19
bar magnet 73
basalt 44
bats, ultrasound 39
batteries
 1, 3, 7, 57
bell jar experiment 37
beta particles/emission
 81, 82, 83, 84, 86, 87
big-bang theory 54, 55
big crunch 55

big spark 13
bill (*electricity not duck or Clinton*) 11
binoculars 30
black dwarf 52
black holes
 51, 52, 55
boiler 79
BOOM! 13
brakes 23, 24
braking distance 24
broken bones 35
broken wrists 75
burglar detectors 3

C
cables, electrical 9
calculating resistance 2
cancer 35, 83
cavity wall insulation
 62, 63
cells 3, 4, 8
chain reaction 86
charges 8, 12, 14
chemical energy 57
christmas fairy lights 5
circuit breaker 76
circuits 1, 4, 8
circular barrier/ripples 27
clothes and blankets 62
clothing crackles 13
clouds of dust 51
coal 66, 67
coil of wire 74, 77
colours 29
comets 48, 50
communications
 30, 33, 49
components 1, 8
compressions 26
conduction, heat
 58, 59, 62, 63
constellations 48
continental drift 44

continental plate 43
continents 42, 43
convection currents
 60, 62
convection, heat
 58, 60, 62, 63
cooking foil 62
cooking food 34
cooling fins 62
Copernicus 48
core 41, 52, 74
cosmic rays 82
cost, domestic electricity 11
cost-effective 63
coulomb 8
cracks, in metal casting 39
cricket, speed of sound 40
critical angle 29, 30
CRO displays 26, 38, 77
crust 43, 44
current-carrying wire 75
current, electrical
 1, 3, 4, 6, 8, 10, 14, 74, 75, 76, 77, 78, 79
curtains 63

D
Dalton, John 85
dangerous 33, 34, 35, 67, 83
data on planets 48
dating of rocks 84
days and seasons 46
DC supply 75
decay, radioactive 86, 87
deceleration 18, 22, 24
definitely uncool 27
dense 29, 52
denser 28, 35, 37
density 41, 60
details swirling around 22
diffraction 31, 33
digital signals 36
diode 3
dispersion 29

dissipated as heat 58
distance-time graphs 18
distance travelled 18
domestic electricity 11
Doppler effect 54
dosage of radiation 35
double glazing 63
drag 21, 22, 23
draught-proofing 63
driving force 1
dust 51, 52, 55
dust removal 13
dynamos 77

E
Earth 47, 48, 52
earthing straps 13
earthquakes 41, 43
Earth's atmosphere
 34, 50
Earth's magnetic field
 44, 73
Earth's orbit 46
Earth's rotation 46
earth wires and fuses 10
eccentric orbits 50
echoes 37, 39
echo questions 40
eddy currents 78
efficiency 65
elastic 57
elastic potential energy
 57, 71
electric bell 76
electric heaters 64
electric motor 75
electrical charge/circuits 8
electrical energy 57
electrical hazards 9
electrical oscillations 38
electrical power 8
electrical pressure 1
electricity 1, 9, 11, 79

Index

electricity meter 11
electrode 14
electrolysis 14
electrolytes 14
electromagnetic devices 76
electromagnetic induction 77, 78
electromagnetic waves/radiation/spectrum 33, 47, 61, 81
electromagnets 74, 76
electrons 1, 12, 13, 14, 59, 81, 85, 86
elliptical orbits 47
EM waves/radiation 32, 33, 47, 81
emissions 67
endoscopes 30, 35
energy dissipation 64
energy flow diagram 64
energy in circuits 8
energy input/output 65
energy of waves 8, 26, 37, 59, 71, 72
energy transfer 57, 64, 65
environment 67
evidence (for plate techtonics) 42, 44
exposure, radiation 35, 83

F

factor of two, echoes 40
feels hotter or colder 59
fibre glass wool 63
filament lamp 2, 3
fingernails 44
fission, nuclear 86
Fleming's left hand rule 75
fluorescent tubes 35
foetus, ultrasound 38, 39
food 57, 71, 83
force 75
force diagrams 19, 21
force of attraction 16, 48
force of gravity 52
forced convection 60
formulae 32
formula triangle 17
fossil fuels 66, 67
fossils 42
fossils, dating of 84
free electrons, in metals 59
free-fallers, terminal velocity 22
frequency of waves 26, 28, 31, 32, 34, 38, 54
friction 12, 21, 23, 71
fuel filling nightmare 13, 57
funny old stuff 55
fuse ratings 3
fuses 10

G

galaxies 51, 54
gamma sources/emission 35, 81, 82, 83, 84, 86, 87
gas 67
generators 77, 79
geographic poles 73
geostationary satellites 49
geothermal energy 69, 70
glass block demo 28
glorified steam engines 86
gradient 2, 18
grain shoots 13
graph, for half life 87
gravitational potential energy 57, 72
gravity 16, 21, 22, 48, 50, 51, 52, 55, 69
greenhouse effect 67
grim up North 24
gripping facts 51

H

half-life 84, 87
harmful/harmless 33, 34, 35
hazards 9, 24, 83
hearing 38
heat 51
heat energy 47, 52, 57, 58, 60, 61, 64
heating 33
heat radiation 34, 61, 62
heat transfer 58, 62, 63
heat when a current flows 8
heat will flow 58
height 72
helium nuclei 81, 86
hideously easy 16
high doses 35, 83
household electrics 6
Hubble telescope 50
hydroelectricity 68

I

Iceland 44
ignore it at your peril 23
image, in plane mirror 27
incidence, angle of 27, 28
India 42
induced voltage 77
induction, electromagnetic 77, 78
inescapable conclusion 54
information 30
infra-red (or IR) 29, 34, 57, 61
inkjet printer 13
input energy 64
instant regurgitation 25
insulating materials 12
insulation 62, 66
insulators 59, 62
iodine 84
ionisation 81, 83
iron 44
iron core 74, 75, 76, 78
iron rocker 76
Isaac Newton 19

J

jet aircraft 40
jigsaw fit 42
joules 11, 57, 71, 72
Jupiter 47, 48

K

kHz (kilohertz) 32
kill cells, radiation 34, 83
kilowatt-hours 11
kinetic energy 24, 57, 58, 71, 72

L

laminated iron core 78
law of reflection 27
laws of motion, three 19
LDR 3
le miserable eternity 55
life cycle of stars 52
lift force 21
light 26, 27, 31, 40
light dependent resistor. *See* LDR
light energy 57
lightning 13, 40
live cricket 40
live wire, in plug 10
loft insulation 62, 63
longitudinal waves 26, 37, 41
long wavelength radio 31
losses, energy 64
loud noise, amplitude 37
loudspeakers 3, 57, 76
lower doses 35, 83

Index

low polar orbit satellites 50
lubricants 23

M
machine efficiency 65
magma 44
magnetic field 73, 74, 75, 76, 77
magnetic polarity 44
magnetic reversal patterns 44
mains electricity 9
main sequence star 52
mantle 43
Mars 47, 48, 53
mass 16, 48, 72
mass balance 16
mass number 85
matt black, surfaces 62
maximum speed 22
media, for waves 28, 29, 33, 37, 39, 61
Mercury 47, 48
metals 14, 59, 62
MHz (1 megahertz) 32
microwaves, ovens 34
mid-Atlantic ridge 44
Milky Way galaxy 51
mines, radiation 82
molten lava 41
moons 48, 49
moths in mid-flight 39
motor, motor effect 3, 75
mountains 43, 44
movement energy 57
mutant cells, cancer 83

N
narrow gap, diffraction 31
national grid 79
natural convection 60
natural gas 66

natural satellites 49
Neptune 47, 48
neutral wire, in a plug 10
neutrons 85, 86
neutron star 52
newton meter 16
newtons 16
nickel 76
night vision 34
non-metals 59, 62
non-renewables 66, 67
normal, light rays 27, 28
northern hemisphere 46
nuclear 67
nuclear energy/fuel 57, 66
nuclear fission/bombs 86
nuclear fusion 52
nuclear power 67
nuclear radiation 81
nuclear reactors 67, 86
nuclear waste 82
nucleus/nuclei 85, 86, 87

O
oceanic plate 43
oceanic trench 43
oil 66, 67
optical fibres 30, 35
orbits 16, 47, 48, 49, 50, 51
overhead cables 12

P
"Pangea" 43
paper rollers 13
parachute 22, 23
parallel circuits 1, 6, 7
partly chewed mouse 25
Pd 4, 6
peak demand 69
peculiar movement of the planets 48
penetration, radiation 81
periscopes 30
permanent magnets 75
perspex 29

photocopier 13
pitch, sound waves 38
plane mirror 27
planetary nebula 52
planets 47, 48, 49, 51, 53
plane waves 27
plate boundaries 43, 44
plates 42, 43, 44
plate tectonics 42
plotting compass 74
plug wiring 9
plum pudding 85
Pluto 47, 48
pockets of air, insulation 62
pollution 66
polythene rod, static 12
potential difference. See Pd
potential energy 72, 73
power 70, 79
power loss 79
power ratings 11
power, sources of 66
power stations 67, 79
power supply 3, 4
pre-natal scanning 38
primary coil 78
prisms 29, 30
proton number 85
protons 85, 86
protostar 52
pump 60
P-waves, seismic waves 41
pylons and cables 79

Q
quality control 38

R
radiant heat 57
radiation hazards 83
radiation, heat 33, 58, 61, 62, 63

radiation, nuclear 51, 81, 82, 83, 84, 86, 87
radiation sickness 83
radiators 62
radio waves 31, 33, 53
radioactive elements 69
radioactivity, radio-isotopes 70, 84, 86, 87
radiographers, X-rays 35
radiotherapy 83
radon gas 82
rainbows, dispersion 29
rarefactions, waves 26
reaction forces 20, 21
real horrors 47
rectangular glass block 28
red giant 52
red-shift 54
reflection 26, 27, 33
refraction 26, 28, 29, 41
relay 76
remote controls, for tv 34
renewables, fuels 66
repelling 12, 73
resistance 2, 4, 6, 79
resistance force 22
resistors 3, 8
resultant force 19, 22
reverberation 37
ridiculous idea 19
ripples 26
ripple tank 27, 28, 31
robots 53
rocks 42
rock strata 42
rotation, of Earth 46
rubber bands 57
Rutherford's scattering 85

Index

S

safety 83
San Andreas Fault 43
San Francisco 43
satellites 49, 50
satellite transmissions 34
Saturn 47, 48
scientific research 35
sea floor spreading 44
seasons 46
secondary coil, transformer 78
second generation stars 52
security marks 35
seismic waves 26, 41
seismographs 41
semiconductor diode 3
series circuits 1, 4, 5
SETI 53
shallower water 28
shock, electrical 12
shock waves 26, 41
sideways vibrations 26
SI units 32
silvered finishes 62
skidding 23
skin cancer 35
skulking cat 17
skydiver 22
slightly tricky formula 72
slinky spring 26
slippy roads 24
slip rings, generator 77
snotty remains 52
solar energy 69, 70
solar system 47, 48, 50, 51
solenoid 73, 74
sonar 39, 40
sound 31, 32, 37, 38, 40
sound energy 57
sound waves 26, 37, 39
South America 42, 43
southern hemisphere 46
Spanish inquisition 48
spark 12, 13
speakers 76
spectrum 33
speed 17, 18, 24, 32, 72
speed of sound 40
spray painting 13
spread 44
spring balance 16
springs 57
spying 49
standard test circuit 1
stars 47, 48, 51, 52
starting pistol, sound 40
static charges 12, 13
static electricity 12, 13
steady speed 18, 19, 21, 22
steady state theory 54
steel, magnetically hard 74
step-down/step-up transformers 78, 79
sterilisation 35
stopping distances 24
stored energy 57
streamlined 23
strength of electromagnets 74
subduction zone 43
Sun 46, 47, 51, 52, 57, 61, 82
sunbeds, uv rays 35
sunburn 34
supernova 52
surface colour/texture 58, 61
survival blankets, silvered 62
S-waves, seismic waves 41
symmetrical pattern 44

T

tectonic plates 42, 43, 44
temperature detectors 3
tension 21
terminal velocity 22
testing components 1
the big crunch 55
thermal energy 57
thermistor 3
thermos flask 62
thermostatic controls 63
thermostats 3
thinking distance 24
three laws of motion 19, 20
thrust 21
thunder and lightning 40
thyroid gland 84
tidal barrages 69
toasters and grills 34
toss big boats around 26
total internal reflection 29, 30
total resistance in circuits 4, 6
tracers in medicine 84
transformers 78, 79
transverse waves 26, 41
treatment of cancer 83
trench 43
turbines 68, 69, 79
turns 74, 75, 77, 78
tv and radio waves 33
twilight zone 46
types of energy 57
tyres and the road 23

U

ultrasonic detection 39
ultrasound 38, 39
ultraviolet light 35
units of electricity 11, 32
universe 51, 54, 55
unstable nuclei 87
uranium 86
Uranus 47, 48
uv rays 35

V

vacuum 33, 37, 61
variable resistor 1, 3
velocity 17
velocity-time graphs 18
Venus 47, 48
vibration energy (heat) 59
vibrations 26, 38
V-I graphs, electricity 1
visible light 31, 35, 36
volcanoes 43, 44
voltage 1, 4, 6, 8, 12, 77, 78, 79
voltmeter 1, 3, 4, 7
volts 1

W

waste energy, heat 64, 78
watts 71
wave formulae 32
wavelength 26, 28, 31, 32, 33
wave power 69
waves 26, 61
weather satellites 50
Wegener's theory 42
weight 16, 20, 21
white dwarf 52
wind power/turbines 68
wires 2
wood burning 68, 70
work done 70, 71

X

x-rays 35

Z

zzzzzzzzzzz 17